THE BUTCHER'S BOOK

HENDRIK DIERENDONCK
RENÉ SÉPUL
MARIJKE LIBERT
STEPHAN VANFLETEREN
THOMAS SWEERTVAEGHER
PIET DE KERSGIETER

DIERENDONCK

FOR RAYMOND

HANNIBAL

WHEN I WAS FOUR, I ALREADY KNEW IT: I WAS GOING TO BE A BUTCHER! I LEARNED EVERYTHING ABOUT MEAT FROM MY FATHER AND MOTHER. BUT MORE THAN ANYTHING IT WAS THE

PASSION

THEY SHOWED IN PURSUING THEIR CRAFT, AND THEIR DEEPLY FELT RESPECT FOR THE TERROIR, THAT MADE ME WHO I AM TODAY: A BUTCHER WITH A VISION.

PASSION, TERROIR, CRAFTSMANSHIP AND TASTE HAVE ALWAYS BEEN THE GUIDING PRINCIPLES IN EVERYTHING I DO; WITHOUT THEM, THE REST DOESN'T MAKE ANY SENSE. I ALSO STARTED MAKING THIS BOOK WITH THOSE VALUES FIRMLY IN MIND. TO HELP REALISE A FUTURE OF LESS BUT BETTER MEAT, THIS IS MY ODE TO ALL THE BREEDERS WHO DO THEIR WORK WITH A DEEP RESPECT FOR ANIMALS AND FOR NATURE. THEY KNOW THE POWER AND BEAUTY OF THE

TERROIR

AND OF THE LAND, AND OF THE FARM ANIMALS.

AT THE SAME TIME, THIS BOOK IS MY TRIBUTE TO ALL THE MEN AND WOMEN OF THE

CRAFT

THE BUTCHERS, THE 'CHARCUTIERS', THE CARVERS – WHO DAY AFTER DAY, HIDDEN FROM VIEW, WITHIN FOUR WALLS, IN THE COLD – PROCESS THE MEAT THAT WE EAT. THEY ARE SKILLED ARTISANS WHO ARE PROUD OF THE HARD WORK THEY DO AND RECEIVE FAR TOO LITTLE APPRECIATION FOR IT.

COOKS AND BUTCHERS NEED TO HONOUR, VALUE AND APPRECIATE THE ANIMAL THAT WAS SLAUGHTERED FOR PREPARATION IN THE KITCHEN, AND RESPECT THE FARMER WHO BREEDS THE ANIMAL.

TASTE

COMES FROM TASTING THE PURENESS OF A PRODUCT WHILE PAYING HOMAGE TO ITS ORIGINS, TO THE SOURCE AND THE PROCESSING. CAMOUFLAGING THOSE THINGS IS OUT OF THE QUESTION. TASTE INVOLVES BOTH RECOGNITION AND ACKNOWLEDGMENT.

WITH THIS BOOK, I HOPE AT THE VERY LEAST TO PASS ON SOME OF MY KNOWLEDGE OF, AND SOME OF MY LOVE FOR, THE PROFESSION THAT MEANS SO MUCH TO ME. ONLY BY SHARING OUR PASSION AND KNOWLEDGE WILL THIS BEAUTIFUL CRAFT SURVIVE AND – I HOPE, AND SOMETIMES ALREADY SEE HAPPENING – IMPROVE AGAIN.

HENDRIK DIERENDONCK

PASSION

TERROIR

CRAFT

TASTE

Marché Traditionnel
Ville de BRIVE
1.04.2014
Foire Primée aux Veaux de Lait
1er PRIX D'EXCELLENCE
ACHETEUR
LEZAY 2014
GRAND PRIX D'HONNEUR
GENISSES
AUTRES RACES & CROISEES

DIERENDONCK. THE NAME WAS A GIFT, THE CRAFT WAS OBTAINED THROUGH HARD WORK, FIRST BY FATHER, THEN BY SON.

THE NAME DIERENDONCK STANDS FOR BEING A REAL BUTCHER, WITH CLEAVER, KNIFE AND 'PÉTRIN'.BUT IT ALSO PERSONIFIES THE BURNING WISH TO KNOW THE PRODUCT, ON THE FARM, AT THE BREEDER'S, AMONG THE 'MARCHANDS'. HENDRIK, THE 'KLIENEN' (AKA 'THE LITTLE GUY'), IS SEEKING PURE FLAVOUR, "THE PATH ALONG WHICH EMOTIONS AND MEMORIES ARE TRANSMITTED". HE IS THE MAN WITH THE HARD-MUSCLED HANDS AND THE SOFT HEART, WHO IS MOVED WHEN HE LOOKS AT HIS SHOP WINDOW, HIS ATELIER, THE COLD ROOMS, THE CURING CHAMBER. PROUD OF HIS CRAFT. FILLED WITH

PASSION

IT'S WHAT EVERYTHING REVOLVES AROUND.

F.DICK
Made in Germany
ROSTFREI

THE CRAFT, HANDED DOWN FROM FATHER TO SON

WAKING UP

HEARING KNOCKS DOWNSTAIRS,

sounds, echoes, commotion. The chopping block is sanded down, the knife is whetted, and then the first chop, *crack*, the first steak or cutlet, and another: *whack*. A little later, the rattle of the shutters going up. Hendrik hears his papa say 'good morning' to someone outside, in the still dusky fresh morning air. The father checks the display counter, his boutique, his shop window. He hopes that the meat will sell well and that it will taste good at the customers' homes later. That's what he does it all for. The sea is still a dark void, light is dawning from the east, an early customer dawdles in front of the door. The child Hendrik, smelling of soap, goes down the stairs, into the shop, eats a first sandwich in the kitchen next door, with freshly made mince. Papa sells his first slice of pâté and waves his son off to school. Later, the father hopes; later, the son thinks.

Hendrik: "It means a lot to grow up in a business where private and work life mingle, downstairs from the living room. You'd walk through the shop to go to school; in the afternoon you'd go through the shop to the back for a hot meal. You'd also go through the shop in the evening to play outside. *Hey!* they sometimes called, you're walking over my clean floor. Raymond Dierendonck's butcher's shop was a household name in Sint-Idesbald – you could feel that even as a child. For us it also meant growing up with the familiar sounds of the knife, the mixing machine, the chopping block, the cleaver. I'm sorry about my children not hearing that any more, the sound of the chopping block being sanded down, there's something really magical about it. I also remember family moments, when, all of a sudden in the evening, the hob would be fired up. Papa makes his way downstairs to the refrigerator, and comes back with a few chipolata sausages. He throws them on the fire. It's an instant party, just like that in the middle of the week: fresh *saucisses* sizzling on the grill right before your eyes.

¶ "You grow up and start being given light chores. *Schuttels kusjen*, cleaning the dishes. You like other jobs better. 'Sticking in' the meat after closing time is one of them. Your parents and the staff act a bit silly then because they let their hair down after another hard day's work. You get infected by their enthusiasm. Once the shutters are closed, the radio is turned on. You can play your own music too, later. Listening to AC/DC, you tidy up the trays and carefully place the meat in the fridge. You see tiredness in your father's face, and also see that he is already secretly longing for the next day. I see myself doing the same thing now, a generation later. I enjoy it when everything is top-notch, freshly made, when the meat and dishes are positioned correctly, no gaps anywhere, no crooked trays, all the labels lined up straight and neat. It has to be *just so* for the Dierendoncks. The shop window is a 'sweet shop', a paradise full of prepared food, but also a carefully considered composition. I acquired expertise and passion through my roots, because I was allowed to experience it."

¶ Spring 2015. Father Raymond is still actively involved in the now much larger and newly conceived shop. He puts on the apron; he's selling today. Hendrik runs back and forth. A little nudge there, a piece of meat in between here, just putting everything right. There's a glow in Hendrik's and Raymond's eyes – is this the kick? "No, getting it ready is not the kick," the father answers, "The kick is when a hundred people are standing in the shop." Hendrik adds: "The kick is seeing our customers leaving here *satisfied*. You showcase your work in the window for them. You've done a great job, you have selected the purest meat from the farmer, the breeder, at the market in Paris or elsewhere; pork, lamb and beef. You've chosen the best methods for transforming the meat into a final product. It would be inappropriate if you just plopped that meat down, without any vision, organisation or proper attention. You have to close the circle."

¶ The circle is closed, the craft has been handed down from Dierendonck father to Dierendonck son, including recipes, wisdom, actions, unbridled commitment, as well as love and boldness. Only one thing is different. Hendrik doesn't live above the shop.

Hendrik: "The living room of days past has become an office. Gone are the sleeping areas for parents and children, and the rows of bunk beds on the third floor where our 'summer guests', the seasonal workers, stayed. Up to a dozen extra people would work here during the holiday months, peak season, and most of them slept there. They were often boys from the country, apprentice butchers. In the evening, we'd sit *ollemolle toope*, crowded together, watching television. It didn't bother me, the crowding, all of the people together. It's just how I grew up. When I was ten, I was already allowed to join in the simple work, such as making sausages or hamburgers."

¶ It wasn't an obligation, father Raymond never made him do anything. His approach to encouraging his son Hendrik's enthusiasm for the work was "not to burn him". Forcing him was out of the question. Calling the 15-year-old out of bed at 6am and making him work 12-hour days would have backfired. In Hendrik, they quietly fanned the flames. Raymond saw that the fire was there, that was enough. He saw it in the way Hendrik's eyes flickered when a new beef carcass was carried in, the way he would stand by his father, looking with admiration at that enormous beast. Raymond had the knife in hand, the boy not yet. He had to wait, and waiting fanned his ardent desire.

Hendrik: "I still remember the exact moment when I was allowed to bone a pork belly for the first time. 'Here,' my father suddenly said. He pushed a stepping stool up to the table because I was short. He handed me a boning knife that was already a bit worn and showed me how to do it one last time. I must have boned hundreds of pork bellies since then. Starting with the basics is essential. That's how you learn the craft. All the while, you yearn for the moment when the big cleaver will also finally be in your hand. Father was a strict taskmaster, he set the bar high. He told me to treat the meat with respect. The animal was not only a precious commodity, the animal had 'given' itself for us. That is why not even one piece was allowed to be wasted. It was a matter of respect and professional pride. Later, my father and I were both horrified by mass production and the industrial meat-processing plants where meat was handled carelessly. In mass production, there is no room for finesse. Too much is thrown away in today's world. Not at Dierendonck; every gramme of meat is worth its weight in gold here."

¶ Raymond Dierendonck wasn't born into a butcher's family. His father was a greengrocer who owned four cows, milked them himself and then went on the milk round, in Middelkerke. Raymond was not university-minded and he went to the butchers' school instead. The story repeated itself in the next generation.

¶ Hendrik was 16, a boy from the seaside, athletic, muscular and hard, doing tricks on his skateboard, but above all… small. He was – and still is – called our *klienen*: little guy. At 16, he was fed up with the traditional schools, Veurne college, Annuntiata Veurne. He grew sick of the comments: "Hendrik can't sit still", "Hendrik can't settle", "Hendrik can't concentrate". Hendrik became discouraged and even started thinking "I'm just stupid." Father Raymond could see himself reflected back in his son. Hendrik decided to go to the butchers' school, KTA Diksmuide. That school had a bad smell about it; it was the end of the line for the *riftje raftje* (riff-raff).

Hendrik: "Still, there were guys who were there with genuine motivation, and we also had a few good teachers. Some of them had worked in my father's shop. But all in all, I still learned more at home and at trade fairs, from the farmers and breeders. I was not being stimulated at school."

¶ In Hendrik's mind, there is a caesura in his life; a turning point when he was 16/17. That's when one day something happened in and around him, a bright moment that is still a wonderful memory.

Hendrik: "It was during the Easter holidays. I was in the middle of boning yet another pork belly and suddenly thought: I feel something, I know I'm *bossing it*, I can do this. My father saw it immediately. Something had changed in me, something to do with insight and maturity. I got the hang of it, literally and figuratively; I became confident and responsible and I enjoyed it, the cutting, the busyness around me, the buzz in the atelier, the rush hour in the shop. It was as if I was transcending myself – without making it a big deal. My father proceeded to give me new things to try, to experiment with. Often I would stumble and fall, a bit like the boy on a skateboard who learns his skill by flipping a hundred times, who gets up again and again, fall after fall, and keeps going until he's mastered that trick. You do marvel at how deep inside you something suddenly evolves – just when something is maturing in your body as well. Becoming a man and becoming a butcher at the same time. I became hungry for knowledge, for the how, the what and the where of the animal. I no longer saw the thighs, the chops, the minced meat and the sausages. More than the pieces, I wanted to see the whole picture, the whole process – including the breeding of the animals, that ultimate foundation of the quality. My father and I went to France together to pick up a stud bull to put with the cows at home. My father had set his sights on a new breed, the West Flemish Red. There was less yield than from the Belgian Blue cows that all the butchers swore by at the time. Dierendonck was synonymous with eccentricity. Both my parents urged their children, above all, to not act like everyone else. Their motto was *niet in de reke lopen* (don't walk in line); don't be one of the crowd, never follow others unthinkingly, but stand out, deliver a quality product and always do your best – *je goeste doen*. My brother is the same in his profession. He is a top-class architect. He chose his path wisely and passionately, never following the beaten path. Finding your own path and always striving for the best is deeply ingrained in both of us."

¶ Choosing your own path does not mean denying the basics. They are sacred. One basic product is the foundation for every butcher, also at Dierendonck. "Everything starts with the *gekapt* – the minced meat."

Hendrik: "The minced meat and the sausages, they are the calling card of a good butcher. My father developed this recipe himself, and the ground meat is still made the way it was on the first day he started his business. The composition of meat, pepper, salt and spices has never changed. The secret is to use pure pork meat, from bellies and shoulders that have been neatly trimmed, all clean, the little tendons removed, then properly grind it to a nice texture with no smearing. Is it a secret recipe? Hmm, we Dierendoncks are not very good at being secretive. But we do have some family recipes: the pâté, for instance: 80% of the visitors to our shop take a slice of pâté with them. It almost counts as cultural heritage in Sint-Idesbald."

¶ After completing his studies, Hendrik struck out to learn new things and travelled all around Belgium to perfect his craft elsewhere. In the meantime, he had also found true love. Evelyne and Hendrik have been together since they were 17. Evelyne was training to be a beautician, but showed up in the butcher's shop one day as a jobbing student.

Hendrik: "I can still picture her, the way she was pricking into a chicken fillet that first day. Not towards herself but away. There was still a lot to learn. Evelyne always understood me, and my ambition, she's also seen how obstinate I became, maybe she's even sometimes silently cursed my agitated experiments, my almost maniacal perseverance. We took some steps of the journey together, even apprenticed together with a butcher in Brussels. We had a very difficult time for a while there, we suffered together. That's also an inevitable part of this job, suffering. We were working in the cold, in the wet, with frozen pig's blood, with *burst* fingers. In the meantime, we were appalled at what we were seeing, and that's when I fully realised that I had my own completely different vision of the profession.

¶ "Evelyne comes from a family of independent tradesmen; her father was an electrician. My father had once actually seen her as a toddler in a playpen in the living room, when he went to pay his lease money to Evelyne's grandfather, Remi Vandromme. Papa later often said: 'I never thought that was my future daughter-in-law sitting in that box.' Vandromme had been a butcher. My mother-in-law, Evelyne's mama, was the butcher's daughter and used to deliver the meat on her bicycle. She cycled on the hard dirt roads of Sint-Idesbald (more dunes than village at the time), and delivered packages of meat to Mrs So-and-So and Madam Whatsit. At that time, the 'beautiful people' would come to stay in Sint-Idesbald, remarkable figures such as the painter Paul Delvaux. Evelyne's grandfather remembers that Delvaux once had no money to pay for his meat. He asked if he could pay with a painting. Oh, never mind that, Remi said. So, because of his generosity, he missed out on a small fortune! Vandromme closed his business and Papa rented the shop. At the back, where Carcasse restaurant is now located, the Hotel Astrid once stood, run by Evelyne's great-grandmother. And now everything has come full circle. Vandromme's granddaughter married a Dierendonck. How lucky we are to bear that name. A teacher once looked up the etymological origin. *Donk* means wading place for animals, but has another meaning too. A *donk* used to be a type of barn: its roof was covered with a thick layer of manure so that the animals had a warm shelter inside. I think that's quite appropriate for our work."

¶ Raymond Dierendonck likes to listen as his son talks enthusiastically, in the kitchen of the Sint-Idesbald shop, where Hendrik is keeping an eye on both the shop and the atelier. Raymond sometimes throws in a comment or two. It never ceases to surprise him, he says, the boost that the name Dierendonck received, and the national and international fame that came from the things Hendrik did to draw the public's attention to good meat and good craftsmanship.

¶ One time, a car full of customers from Limburg was parked on the doorstep at eight in the morning; they bought enough meat to fill their freezers and then drove straight back home again.

Raymond: "The fact that people come this far for our authenticity really moves me. I may have built the foundations, but Hendrik has developed the story and put it out into the world, in a different era but with the same drive as I had, the same spirit, and through hard work. I saw the talent emerge, I saw how Hendrik was watching when I was up to my armpits mixing the pâté in the *pétrin*. He'd also often stand on a bench in the shop. I would ask him, as a joke, in front of the customers, 'And, boy, what do you want to be when you grow up?' 'Farmer's pâté!' he would answer, 'I want to be a farmer's pâté'." Raymond laughs loudly and heads to the shop. "I want to show you something." He returns, lays the cleaver on the table; the original knife from that time, bought in the 1970s, still the Knife with a capital K. It lies as well in the father's hand as in the son's hand. It's as if their fingers grew around it, their hands melding to the handle.

Hendrik: "I can't explain how that feels. The knife just fits. Everything is just right, the weight, the height, the heft and the swing. We're now having another cleaver made by a knife specialist in Tel Aviv. We let him measure this knife, calculate the weight, we want the swing to be the same. A prototype has been made, but still needs more work, we're not fully feeling it yet. (*Hendrik grasps the old cleaver in his hand*) How much meat do you think has already seen the sharp side of this blade? We couldn't make a guess within 100 kg. The knife is sacred and papa still sharpens it himself, with the whetting stone: a craft in itself. Commitment first, revenue second, that is what it's all about. If earning cash is the only aim, things go wrong at some point. Of course, we need to get some income after the hard work, but our highest goal is to please our customers."

Raymond: "Those customers are our real weapons. They reflect who we are, how we exist, and what our character is. The shop assistants also know that and they are trained to provide good customer service. Each customer is treated personally and equally, whether it's a big shot or the little old lady who comes to get her 100 g of *préparé* every day. And if someone asks for a marrow bone, we give it away. It's not the kind of thing you charge money for, is it? You shall truly receive only when you've learned to give." ❧

THE LITTLE GUY MAKES SACRIFICES AND STEPS UP

NO,

THEY DID NOT ENTHUSE HIM, the internships that Hendrik did as an apprentice butcher, in various Flemish cities and in the capital, didn't inspire him. It became apparent that he has a completely different view of the profession. Nevertheless, the lessons learned elsewhere were useful; now he knew how he didn't want to do it. His vision of the 'good' craft became clearer and clearer, as did his pride in being a Dierendonck who chooses quality every time, to the point of an obsession.

¶ One day he had to grapple with bad news; another caesura in Hendrik's life. One of his loved ones, someone with whom he has a special bond, became seriously ill. Terminally ill even. It caused fear, but it also changed his outlook on life. "During that time, I started to really think about the value of life, and of family, and about the need to be a passionate person, with the need to do something."

¶ It was not the first time he had been confronted with a serious illness. When he was two, he himself had balanced on the border between life and death. "It was in the summer, a day with lovely weather. My brother and I went to the beach with the nanny. On the way I quite suddenly took a turn for the worse, with acute diarrhoea that just wouldn't stop. Sick as a parrot, I was carried home. An hour later, I was in hospital – the diagnosis was dehydration of the abdominal wall after a viral infection. It wasn't at all clear if I would make it. After a short period of uncertainty, I recovered. Mama felt the after-effects, though. She had had a big shock, a traumatic experience: for the first time she had felt that terrible fear that she might lose a child. My brother and I were surrounded equally with love and care, but a tiny bit more attention went to me, mama's trouble child, mama's *keppe*. Later, it also turned out that the stomach dehydration was the reason for my stunted growth. I would be our *klienen* forever."

¶ "The bad things I experienced, the downward spiral of the profession, my exasperation, I decided to let it all go, to stop wasting my time but instead take matters into my own hands." Hendrik was then 23 and this was a pivotal moment. "I was ready to start the real work, building on the foundation that had been laid. And so suddenly, one day, my question came straight out: 'Papa, I would like to take over the butcher's shop.' I saw my father start, it took him by surprise, his own fire was still burning bright. But he agreed with my plan. I did wonder later if he had stopped too soon. On the other hand, he didn't really stop. He kept working in the business, threw himself passionately into the breeding of the West Flemish Red cattle, and supported me in everything I did – even though sometimes he was also looking at me like '*What's that geezer getting up to now?*' I went abroad in search of the best meat. Week after week, I would spend half the night and a morning restlessly roaming the most historic meat market in Europe: Rungis in Paris. I also travelled to remote locations across Europe in search of the best beasts."

¶ The butcher's shop in Sint-Idesbald underwent a radical change three years after the takeover. "I had a clear plan. The renovation was by no means smooth sailing. I ended up in an architectural and legal hornets' nest. It took up a lot of energy that I needed for other things. I had been hoping to make the transition in one year. It took three. During the transition period we were working in containers next to the construction site. A sea container became the freezer, a long construction site container stored our material, the cutter, the sausage stuffer, and the third container was the atelier. My God, we really had to overcome some challenges in those years."

¶ The new butcher's shop was finally built and really showed Hendrik's signature. It had to be something extraordinary, an expression of his ideals, an illustration of his concept. The magic word: transparency. Hendrik literally made the workplace transparent, a first in the butchering world.

Hendrik: "I want to show the customer how everything is prepared, the work we do with our basic products. Cutting the meat, preparing the dishes, everything has to be out there for everyone to see. This was a revolutionary step to take, a contrary choice too, at a time when the food industry was trying to hide as much as it could. I pulled the curtains apart and let them look behind the scenes. I also wanted to stand up and show myself."

¶ Hendrik and his stature. It runs through our conversations like a red thread, as an aside, as a descriptor. "Because of his build…," Raymond will say. "Because I was a *klienen*," Hendrik mixes into his narrative. The influence of physiology was clearly important in the development and expansion of Dierendonck.

Hendrik: "The fact that I am small in stature certainly played a role in what I wanted to achieve in my professional life. It made me develop more personality, more daring. I'd raise my voice, literally stick my neck out, and that's all related to my posture. As a child I was put on a tray in the shop; as a young adult I often had to push my way into company to make myself visible. All of this fuelled the need to say: 'I am here, look at what I've learned, what I know and can do.'"

¶ Paris, at a culinary event for up-and-coming talent, just at the point when Hendrik was gaining maturity as the new owner of the business. *Le petit Belge* has been invited to give a demo. Place of action, a back room.

Hendrik: "I came in with two full carts of meat, everything stacked on hay. Outside I had to squeeze my way through the crowd, in the hall itself there was no one to be seen. I could feel it on my back that I was attracting attention. People slowly trickled in, curious about that little guy with his farm carts. A well-known chef from New York started taking pictures. A few more foreigners gathered around me. The chef of The Jane restaurant gave a demonstration with my products, to what had now become a full hall of people. It wasn't just a gimmick, of course. I had brought the finest products with me and told my story about the origin of the meat. I also showed my emotion. Emotion is a major component of the Dierendonck story, including my father's."

¶ Father Raymond – not a giant either, but slightly taller and, more importantly, stouter than the lean Hendrik – agrees that *the little guy carved out a place for himself*, he literally wanted to step up, to rise above.

Raymond: "I think the story that best illustrates this is The Flemish Primitives event sixteen years ago, a fair where a thousand chefs from all over the world were present, but where farmers and producers were also in the spotlight. Hendrik thought of his own original way to draw attention. He came to me and said, 'Papa, I want to go on stage with an animal, to promote your Flemish Red cow, can you take care of that?' I immediately started calling around and found a cow. But how were we going to get the animal, quietly tending to its own business in the meadow or a shed, up on a stage in front of a thousand people? We started preparing as thoroughly as possible. Every day in the stall next to the cow the radio was turned on, first softly and gradually louder, then really loud, beat music and rock. And every day the farmer took the cow for a walk along the street, so that it became accustomed to all kinds of noises, including traffic. The day before the fair we washed the animal, and on the morning of the event it wasn't fed, so that it wouldn't be doing its business on stage. The farmer went along to the fair, wearing a white shirt and a red scarf. The cow was put in a cargo lift in Ostend casino. A thousand kilos, that had also been researched in advance, to make sure the weight would not be a problem. Between the lift and the stage, the farmer talked nonstop into the cow's ear, the familiar voice reassuring the animal so that it remained calm. In the meantime, Hendrik had started his lecture on the quality of this new product for the audience, in flawless English. And then the cow entered the stage, standing majestically behind him like a show model. The planks under the animal creaked but did not break. The greats of the world, Michel Bras and colleagues, couldn't believe their eyes.

Hendrik got their attention and, more importantly: his message was heard, with the animal as exhibit A. After his talk, the cow, farmer and butcher received thunderous applause. The cow was unperturbed throughout."

¶ Hendrik was delighted. Slowly but surely, he was reaching experts as well as gaining an ever-widening audience with his speeches about terroir, passion and craft. Meanwhile, consumers were finding their way to the western corner of the country: they came from Kortrijk, from Tongeren, people drove – and are still driving – back and forth to buy a *côte à l'os* (large sirloin cut on the bone) from Dierendonck.

Hendrik: "Success also has a downside: you're creating increasingly higher expectations. I want to keep rising to meet them. Colleagues tell me we are trendsetters, but I don't like to hear that because I associate trends with something temporary. I don't want this to be a passing fad. Colleagues in the trade are also starting to use my terminology – such as terroir. I see that some are offering better quality and a greater diversity of meat in their butcher's shops. In the meantime, I have to keep going and keep innovating, in terms of technology, craftsmanship and range. I don't want to get too big for my boots; I don't want to become arrogant because great chefs come to our place. I admit I enjoy the appreciation, but sometimes I miss the groundedness of pure butcher's work. Nothing is more fun after a busy period than joining the crew for work again at six in the morning. Carving meat again, boning a pork belly. It is pure Zen."

¶ The Dierendonck butcher's shop did not supply the restaurant world in the past. Raymond occasionally provided meat for a friend who owned a restaurant, but that was it. The customers who came to the shop were the most important. Until West Flemish Red beef came into the picture, discovered by Raymond and touted by his son on various platforms.

Hendrik: "This beef immediately piqued the interest of Kobe Desramaults, chef of In De Wulf. We got talking and that's how I got to know David Martin from La Paix restaurant. Later, I got a call from Sergio Herman. He introduced himself in his inimitable style: 'Are you gonna come over with some meat?' Apparently his team had been following me for some time on Facebook. They had even sent people to the shop, mystery shoppers. At the time, I'd just opened a new shop in Nieuwpoort, bought a new van and put our new logo on it. So I got the van, packed it with meat, and drove to Sluis. 'Show me your wares, let's have a look,' Sergio said. He couldn't believe his eyes, the cornucopia I had on offer. We talked, tasted. I saw similarities between us. We had both taken over the business from a parent and implemented changes, we had grown, had persisted after hard work and through difficult periods, and had made that obstinate and unconventional choice for craftsmanship and quality. Meeting Sergio, working with him, brought about another breakthrough. The name Dierendonck was suddenly – literally – on the menu of the Oud Sluis. Suddenly everyone was calling us, other chefs and restaurateurs wanted a piece of the action. I sensed I had to be careful and not overdo it. I had once said I wouldn't get into the hospitality sector. In the meantime, we do work with some hospitality ambassadors, but I must continue to cherish our daily customers. Marietje from around the corner, who comes to our shop get her steak, is part of the foundation of the success that led us to these star kitchens. I impress this upon our shop staff, who are at risk of becoming blasé about the fact that people visit us from far and wide to buy meat for up to 200 euros at a time. I say: don't forget our roots, they are the heart of our business. The day you stop honouring the small customer, you lose control and feeling for your business. We must continue to honour traditions, to prepare fresh black pudding on Tuesdays, fresh white sausages on Wednesdays, and so forth. I want to stay humble. I have been on a quest, experimenting and refining the quality and expertise, I've made the entire loop to get back to where I started: the butcher becomes a butcher again, settled once again in his profession. Although the battle continues. Too many young people are still finding out during their internships that not much is left of the real work. The meat comes in wrapped in a plastic vacuum pack, the sauces in separate bags. Pour them out into containers and place them in the display case and you're done. A butcher can start without an atelier – with a large cold room instead – and be buyer and seller in one. At ours, a cow arrives in quarters, we stand before it and discuss it: this piece is meant for that, we'll be doing this with that piece. Then the work in the atelier follows.

¶ "We also need the general public to be more involved in this story. People need to understand more about eating habits. You don't need to eat a kilo of ground beef every day. Eat less meat, but better meat is my motto, and also: bring those taste buds back to life. That's the nature of my quest, and that is why I want to allow the customer to see how we work. Everyone should be able to see that there is no cheating, there are no shortcuts. That the animals are being skinned and chopped, cleaned and boned and that we prepare our daily dishes ourselves. No substitutes, no tricks, it's all real – but almost raised to an art. And in the meantime you make your sacrifices and persevere, stubborn and driven." ❧

THE MOTHER, THE ART

EIGHT O'CLOCK,

IN THE MORNING.

In the Dierendonck atelier, the meat stock bubbles softly on the stove and new potatoes are boiling in wide flat pans. Small pyramids of freshly cut stewing beef are arranged on the tables. This crew has already done two hours of work. Their fine products are placed in the window after inspection by Hendrik. He finishes the arrangement of the 'sweet shop' with the *pièces de résistance*: beef from the curing chamber. Then he has breakfast with his father. Sandwiches with pâté and sliced ham. They check the region and sports pages of their local newspapers amid mumbled exchanges. Raymond asks about Hendrik's plans for the day, then stands up and puts on the apron with the logo of Dierendonck – a cow, what else? "And that second red?" Hendrik asks – "red" for the Flemish Red cattle. "It's taken care of," says Raymond and leaves.
¶ Hendrik beckons. "Come and look, yesterday a lot of beautiful things came in again." Around the corner we enter the no-man's land of the walk-in cold rooms. Hendrik pulls one of the fridge doors open. Inside, the quarters of beef are hanging side by side. "Smell this," he says and sniffs the air himself too. "I smell the hay, and you?"
¶ There's something about the way he looks at it, at the dead animal on a meat hook. As if it's more than just meat, and the hook is more than a thick iron bracket carrying dead weight. As if it were a hook hoisting a different type of project, the creation of a resourceful innovator, an artist.

Hendrik: "Beauty is the first word that comes to mind when I look at these pieces of meat, and respect is the second. The farmer has done everything to ensure that these animals are raised well, to feed them and to provide them with the right environment. Then they were slaughtered, sacrificed as it were. When they are carried inside here, in quarters, I am grateful for the privilege of hanging them in my cold room. The beast has become meat, an array of colour, fat content and structure, but at the same time you can still feel the power somewhere of when the animal was still alive."
¶ That morning we had heard Papa Raymond talk about his "own breeding" with maybe a little less emotion in his voice, but just as much passion. He told us how he bought 16 West Flemish Red cattle from an 80-year-old farmer, and now owns 20 cows of this old breed, some with a bloodline dating back 100 years. He keeps looking for the right stud with the right sperm, he told us with undiminishing enthusiasm. Curious conversations to have on a morning; strange also how the Dierendoncks invariably use terms such as 'creativity' for their craft, while we're talking about animals that, once fattened up, go to the slaughterhouse.
¶ "Hendrik takes more after his mama than me," Raymond suddenly says. "Yes, that streak of creativity. Our other son, an architect, also got that from her. Alexander is a top-grade talent, but he doesn't broadcast his story in public, he doesn't really seek out attention. Hendrik has never had a problem with showcasing himself."

Hendrik: "It's been quite an exploration, but as time passed it has become a positive story, and no longer one of revenge. The need to overcompensate has run its course. The little guy is done with going all out to prove himself, that complex lies far behind me. Looking forwards instead of back, that's what I'm doing. Of course, I carry my personal history with me, the influence of both the diligent father and the artistic mother, that double influx. Mama was a very important factor, much more than she suspects. Her taste was crucial, both in culinary terms, as well as in the sense of beauty. Still, my parents, as they sometimes say, 'each have their child'. I followed in the footsteps of the butcher, my brother followed the artistic mother. The work Alexander designs, invents and makes is focused on good taste and presentation, but above all the right proportions. For him, all concepts must be fulfilled perfectly, well put together, all dimensions have to be just right. And that's how I see it too. Sometimes it is about the details. Look at Carcasse to see how meticulous we are – the chairs, tables, glasses and cutlery. It shouldn't be a little bit perfect, but perfect in every way. 'What are you fussing about?', I sometimes hear people say. I couldn't do it any other way, we didn't learn any other way at home. In the past, the butchers made a little flyer showing their offerings for the holidays. We didn't. Mama designed a booklet, with a menu and beautiful stories. Mama decorated the shop, down to the last detail. There have never been plastic flowers here, never fake ones; always real, always fresh bouquets. 'If you can't have the real thing, better to have nothing,' she said. And that was perfectly matched with what Papa was putting in or taking out of the fridge. I look at our products like actual projects. Of course, I am not making art, but I do feel a kind of connection. Something is stirring in my head, it has to get out, I have to shape it. Fundamentally, it is about idealism, about what you believe in, and about emotion, of course."

¶ Hendrik beckons again and walks past the cold rooms, through the connecting hallway to Carcasse restaurant. In the middle of the shop stands the large curing chamber. Open it, put your head in and sniff. It has a certain aroma, you come to recognise it, you develop your sense of smell here, it's like a cross between hay and grass. Close the cupboard and stand in front of the glass, staring for minutes in silent awe at the meat that hangs there, in its various stages of curing, its many shades of red: vermilion, soft pink, cognac brown. The compositions are fabulous. It could be a work by Jan Fabre, or what the hell, Damien Hirst. But it also looks a bit like the paintings by that old master Joachim Beuckelaer.

¶ Hendrik guffaws: "Speaking about meat and art in the same sentence, it's a bit over the top, isn't it? I think people would say, 'That butcher, he's gone around the twist.' On the other hand, if you are talking about something that is beautiful as well as tasty, why should you not use that word? Do you know what I find really spectacular. The head of the animal, once slaughtered, once the head is separated from its body. You can look at it in so many ways. As butchering waste product, or as something of value. You can put it on a platform, hang a cloth behind it and let the photographer take a photograph. We did that for this book. Stephan and I spent hours looking at a cow's head. First with the spotlights on it, which produced a raw image; then in the shadows, the head radiated power, but then give it a slight turn and suddenly it becomes a vulnerable, sacrificed beast. That feeling that you are master of this beast, but you also feel humble and grateful for what it gives you. That is why, as a butcher, I have to treat the whole animal with respect. Pig, lamb or cow. I have to bone it delicately, clean it, get rid of the sinews and, most importantly, not throw anything away. This is nature that I am working with. With my own two hands too. Butchery is hands-on work, hands that are swollen from the cold and muscled from the work, but never rough. Because they are working with a lot of natural grease, with moisturiser. (*smiles*) My wife says I have soft hands. Most butchers have soft hands. It's strange really, that the hands that chop and cut are so tender at the same time." ❧

CROSSING BOUNDARIES: IS THIS MEAT AGED OR ROTTEN?

NEW IDEAS,

SAYS HENDRIK,

you won't get from your neighbour or the butcher down the street. You will not find new ideas in other display cases in your village, or even the other side of the country. You need to find them away from the familiar terrain. Exploring, on different breeding grounds.

Hendrik: "That's why I travelled from Scotland to Spain and visited all those countries in between. I learned and incorporated new things, not only broadening my knowledge and skills, I also was getting up the nerve to be more daring, to try things out. The pivotal experiment, fourteen years ago, was the aging of beef. They've always done this in England and America. Why don't we do it, I wondered. To ask the question was to embark on this adventure, at first on a small scale. I ignored my father, who frowned, and made comments like: 'Do you really think we can sell that rotten meat?' But no one could put me off my new pursuit. I tried a piece out, first in the regular fridge. Three weeks… that was quite a lot then. Later, I added another week, noting the temperature and humidity, later still a special cupboard was built, and my knowledge continued to grow. At a tasting in Brussels, I sat next to a three-star chef who began to explain to me what aging meat was all about. I almost got into a fight with him. What he was saying was just wrong. Then at home I started pushing against the boundaries of what is tolerable, experimenting again; a few more days, a few more weeks, and yet another kind of beef. It was sheer fanaticism. Sometimes it was a wasted effort, at other times the results were fabulous. Until the moment came that I had completely mastered the process, everything was on point and the sheer enjoyment could begin: that of passing it on to the public. They too became enthusiastic. Now we laugh when we think about that pioneering period, the pitying looks we would get from colleagues – the criticism. Aging meat has become a fashion now. Eating meat aged ten to 12 weeks, nobody gives it a second thought any more. Of course, aging is not about 'the longest time' but about 'the best time' – about flavour, in other words, and that's a personal matter. Just as it is with wine. Some prefer burgundy, others prefer Bordeaux; some like it younger, others older."

¶ Papa Raymond, meanwhile, is a convert. He often stands in front of that dry-aging cabinet just looking, at the pieces of beef that are rotating, suitably cooled, with the correct degree of moisture. Everything inside has been finely calibrated down to the last detail. All kinds of beef are there, and a Dierendonck can immediately identify the beast from the meat: Scottish Highland, Simmental, Limousin.

¶ Hendrik got what he wanted, meat with more character, a more refined flavour, different tenderness. Tried, tasted and true. And he explored boundaries, sometimes crossing them. "The most extreme thing I ever did?" He stalls a little. "Eating meat that had been aged for between 150 and 160 days. That really was starting to reach the edges of rotting, but you also have to explore that when you're growing. Upper limit, lower limit, bottom and ceiling." ❧

DARE TO SHOW YOURSELF, SHOW THE TEARS, THE LIGHT AND THE DARK

QUIET

IS NEVER GOOD, THE SAYING GOES

at the Dierendonck atelier in Sint-Idesbald. Restless is our spirit. If a quiet period looms on the horizon, action must be taken immediately. It was the same in the past, after the hellish summer months, when the shopfront would start showing the wear and tear of the queues of customers. The pressure eased off briefly in autumn, but never for long. It was not Raymond's style to close the shutters, clear out the fridge and spend the remainder of the year sunbathing in Mallorca. After the *coup de feu* (peak summer season) in July and August, he walked around restlessly, wanting to invent something, trying out new things. When all that thinking would yield results, and experimenting would yield a delicious new product, the emotional release was great. Perhaps emotion is the spice that makes the Dierendonck meat range so irresistible.

¶ When father and son take time together to really talk about their life's work, pure emotion often wells up. Papa Raymond will then shift up a gear verbally, talking his feelings away. Hendrik does the opposite. He falters, freezes, his eyes well up. The purest emotion appears. Tears.

Raymond: "The passion for his profession moves him deeply. He's more emotional than I am – no, he shows it differently. It has a lot to do with his boundless commitment. I could not have done it, scouting nights and mornings through Paris, or at markets, in meadows, walking around farms in every corner of Europe, looking at animals and inspecting meat. Then there's the practical organisation: intensive renovations, opening our shops and production centre… It never stops."

Hendrik: "You've got to keep going, you can't hold back when you're expanding. But I also enjoy myself a lot on the road, you know, I let all emotions come, including joy, euphoria. Tears *(falters)*, they come from deep. *Dju*, here I go again. *(pause, then to Raymond)* It could also be tears of anger. Remember, papa, when we went to talk to our fellow butchers, how we sat down afterwards with a sigh, both full of emotion, and said, 'What was that we just heard?' And also: 'What the hell are they doing?' It troubled us. We didn't really fit in. We were the only butcher's shop making real mashed potatoes. 'Come on,' the others would laugh, 'what you are doing, mashed potatoes, you won't make a penny's worth of margin on that.' They took mousseline powder, thickened it with water and put that concoction right on their counter. A Dierendonck becomes acutely uncomfortable then, that really touches his butcher's heart. I really can't do it without being moved, without feeling – whether positive or negative. My emotions are only getting stronger as I get older. You can feel the evolution, of making it after several setbacks, you feel driven to – and have the chance to – spread your story; and what's more, it's about a profession you once were shamed for. When I was a young man, I sometimes went out with my brother. Students would ask me: 'And what do you do?' 'I'm a butcher,' I'd say, self-consciously. Some of them looked at me as if I were a piece of shit. The profession that was once considered inferior has now been upgraded, re-established and widely celebrated. My tears are often an expression of happiness. When I get my hands on a beautiful end product in the atelier, taste it, feel it, see the texture, when I can tell in everything that it's complete, I immediately get emotional too. I think that wiping away a tear is a strength and not, as is often said, an expression of weakness. I really am not half-soft, I work hard for my goals, I don't trample others, I choose my own path, I am quite obstinate."

¶ Ten kilometres from Sint-Idesbald is Dierendonck's second shop, in Nieuwpoort. It is Hendrik's great pride and also a crucial port of call if you want to talk to him about his passions. He's already pointing out the building when we're still on the other side of the street, indicating the facade, and just before entering he bends down, quite unexpectedly, tugging the carpet with 'Dierendonck' printed on it half a centimetre more to the right. "It was crooked, eh?" he says, and laughs, a bit apologetically, as if caught out. Inside, we are warmly welcomed by the salesperson, who does do a quick sprint to the back counter, straightening two more trays, shifting a jar and then looking up proudly. "They know me," Hendrik laughs. "They know that I like a good presentation, everything neat and tidy. They're doing an incredible job here. It makes me very happy."

¶ Commitment and ambition are one thing, but what happens when efficiency becomes a burden, when professionalism leads to perfectionism, when the commitment to excellence leads to maniacal behaviour? Hendrik considers the question, unsure, thinks deeply for a moment and then says, shrugging: "I don't know."

¶ "I wouldn't call it maniacal, it's a pursuit of precision. It's like a photographer waiting for hours for the lighting to be perfect, then developing his prints while wondering all the time if it's come out the way he wanted. I know I shouldn't go overboard, and for now it's still tolerable, but sometimes I need to protect myself and have even more faith in others and let the wonderful people I work with know how much I appreciate them. When I took over the business from my father, four people worked here full time. Now we have a total of a hundred employees working in the ateliers, the six shops and the restaurant. It may sound contradictory, to hold on to your foundations, protect the product, agitate against mass production and yet still expand. Maybe someday I'll run into a wall, but I'm not afraid. The only thing I'm afraid of is losing my family. If everything would suddenly fall apart tomorrow, I know one thing for sure: I'm a good butcher, and I'll continue in that profession with pleasure. What would I hate to lose? I don't know. Money? It has never been an end in itself. Maybe one thing: my cleaver. I would regret that, but that is not irreplaceable either."

¶ "What sometimes scares me is how people see me now. Suddenly, this butcher is on the TV show *Reyers laat* and hears Reyers say: 'Dierendonck has become a household name.' I think: 'Shit man, what's all that.' I was shocked, but at the same time I know that this is the result of what I started. I recently read: 'He is the man who got Flanders to start savouring meat again.' Is that true or not? I think, um, maybe a little bit?" *(smiles)*

¶ "My great fortune has been that I've had the right people around me. Without them, I might have been a scared butcher between his four walls. But I am familiar with them, the walls that surround you, and fear, even agony. My father knows them too. That black beast visits us on a regular basis. We can be feeling good, super-enthusiastic, and all of a sudden it turns, we become gloomy doomsday thinkers. For up to two weeks, we become unapproachable and unreachable, asking ourselves the existential question: 'What are we actually doing?' Maybe it is the repercussions of the hard work or the backlash of the euphoria. Of course, it is also a tough job. I know a load of butchers who have worked themselves to the bone, who are physically broken, have rheumatism from the cold, or arthritis, or broken knees from standing, a broken back from lifting and carrying heavy weights the wrong way. It is a physically demanding profession, but also a profession of strong and proud people. At Culinaria seven years ago, we stood side by side with the guys from our atelier, with our offerings, our products. Chefs came by and whispered, 'Such a beautiful sight, so many personalities together.' A well-known TV chef said to me, 'Together you all radiate power.' I loved that compliment, that we're showing our pleasure in such a way, that those young people were proud to be alongside us, showing the fire that burned. That's the best gift of all. Pride gives strength." ❧

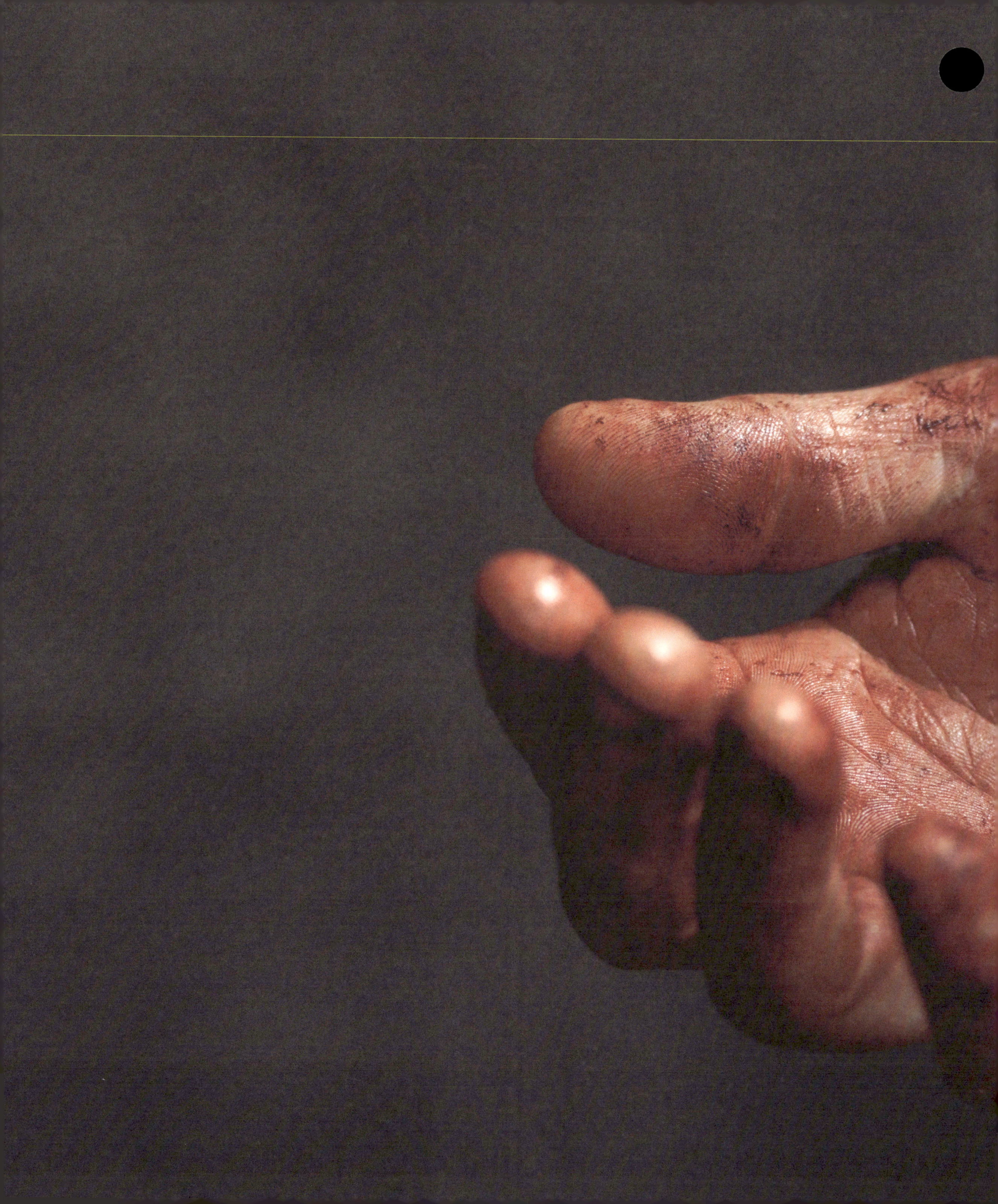

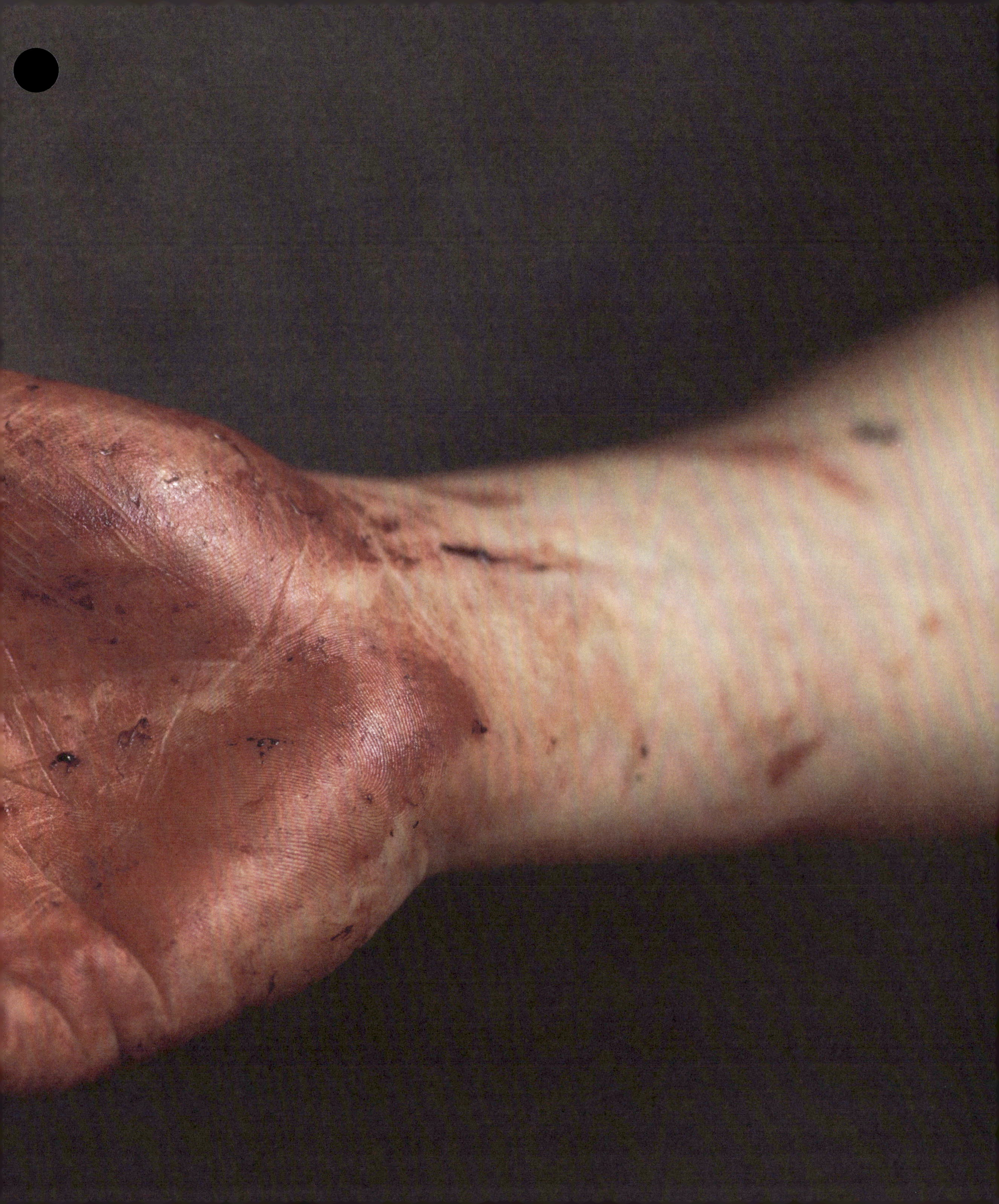

"...SHED FOR YOU AND ALL PEOPLE..."

HENDRIK
IS A BUTCHER,

not the one who does the slaughtering, the meat processing. Not a fan of slitting animals' throats, of killing animals. Is repression the reason? Does he dodge his head out of embarrassment, accepting this is the sacrifice that must be made, it's his work after all, his living, and for the sake of the customer? He shakes his head, no. It has to do with a sort of reverence. Those who slaughter often, he says, tend to get used to it after a while. And if there is one thing he wants to avoid at all costs, it is that it becomes a habit: that killing an animal is experienced as a repetitive act, as something almost businesslike. Hendrik did once do the slaughtering. When he was 18, at the butchers' school in Diksmuide.

Hendrik: "I was the age to want it. I wanted to satisfy my curiosity, to experience the action, so that I would be able to talk about it from my own experience later. Slaughter was a lesson too. How to prepare, how to cut, how to collect the blood, how to clean afterwards. What immediately interested me was the way the killing itself happened. I knew that a bad slaughter produced poorer quality meat. If the animal doesn't suffer, the meat is better. It has a lower pH-level than a traumatised animal. With a high pH, the meat retains more water and acquires a grey cast, which of course has consequences for the butcher and his customer. I can immediately tell how the animal was slaughtered by the structure and wetness of the meat. If the flesh has a shine on it, if the meat gleams, the final stage was not good for the animal."

¶ Slaughtering, killing an animal, is a matter of intense emotion in Hendrik's view. It involves 'making the transition', crossing that thin line between a living and dead animal. And that involves the human being who subjugates the animal.

Hendrik: "The law of the strongest. As a butcher you're also in charge of nature. I've always been highly aware of the fact that a living creature is being sacrificed. This is one of the reasons why I always insist on respect for the meat that ends up on our cutting tables after slaughter. It is not a thing, even if the meat becomes a product in your hands. Anyone who wants to have professional pride in their craft must complete the entire cycle. The killed animal, now made into meat, deserves respect. Also once it is boned, carved, skinned, trimmed or chopped, displayed in the counter, wrapped in paper and on its way home with the customer.

¶ The blood. That too is the butcher's material, his liquid asset. There is no meat without blood, in all its variations of redness, thickness, coagulation and appearance. Dark red and congealed, light coral or vermilion, smudges on the work apron, rivulets meandering over the knife, dried-up blood that crackles between the butcher's fingers. The smell also, that settles in the nose, that sweetish odour, different from animal to animal.

Hendrik: "Cow's blood smells kind of gloomy. The scent of pig's blood is more volatile. When I get fresh meat and hang it in the fridge, I can tell by the aroma what the animals were fed, grass or hay. I can smell whether they lived outside or inside. I smell nature in the meat, or I smell nothing. Plumped meat with water in it smells like nothing. Meat that comes from animals that have been in the cowshed all the time has a musty, dark flavour; well, in a word, it tastes of barn. Cattle who grazed outdoors confirm the cliché of 'happy cow, good meat'. Little lambs from the Pyrénées who frolicked in meadows at an elevation of 1,000 metres smell of liveliness and freshness. You can taste it. I dream of a shop where I

can do meat tastings, according to breed, animal and age. Where I can ask the customer about his or her taste preferences, as the sommelier does with wine, and together determine what will suit their taste buds best. When I tell my fellow butchers this with all of my typical enthusiasm, I get strange reactions. They think I'm pretentious. But really, oh, it just logically follows from what I'm working to achieve, my goal: that people awaken again from the dullness of their palate, that they learn to taste again. Flavour is the path through which emotions and memories are transmitted. What should we do with a next generation that has neglected its senses and thereby squandered some of its memory, history and emotions? *(falters)*. Ah, those tears again, my soft heart. 'The emotional warrior', I was once called in an interview, and I think it's not far off the mark. Serving is also an important word. Giving people the fruits of what you've gathered, discovered and learned. It's about meat, and somehow that sounds trivial, while… it's about opposites: giving life after death, providing good food. It's about mortality and immortality."
¶ "In the light of eternity, what I do is extremely finite, and yet I want to have meant something. I am 47 years old, this is an important moment in my life. I feel a great restlessness as well as a need to finally find some peace. Seldom was I involved in a greater battle with myself, seldom was the energy so highly strung, the need to communicate so great. I spent a long time searching for seeds, preparing the soil and learning the sowing techniques. Now my quest is sprouting and growing and it's time to harvest. And enjoy, of course. The way you can enjoy a good piece of meat – *a goe stiksje vlêes*." ❧

TERROIR

TO HENDRIK DIERENDONCK MEANS FLAVOUR AND VARIETY. IT'S WHAT DISTINGUISHES A LAMB IN THE PYRÉNÉES FROM A LAMB IN QUERCY OR A SALT-MARSH LAMB. IT'S THE FLAVOUR OF THE LANDSCAPE. WHAT YOU SEE WITH YOUR EYES, YOU TASTE IN YOUR MOUTH. IT'S NATURE.

WE GO ON A ROAD TRIP TO TAKE AN INVENTORY OF DIFFERENT TERROIRS. FIRST RUNGIS, THE LARGEST WHOLESALE MARKET IN THE WORLD; THEN THE CORRÈZE, THE ULTIMATE LIVESTOCK FARMING REGION; AND THEN THE PYRÉNÉES, WHERE WE WANT TO LEARN EVERYTHING ABOUT FARMING MILK-FED LAMBS. WE ALSO TALK TO FARMERS IN NEVELE AND STEENVOORDE.
AT HOME, IN BACHTEN DE KUPE, OUR WEST FLEMISH RED AWAITS US...

18
17
16

"YOU HAVE TO BE FAMILIAR WITH THE HERDS, THE BREEDS, THE TERROIRS, AND YOU HAVE TO SHARE THAT KNOWLEDGE WITH YOUR CUSTOMERS."

Tuesday 4pm – Departure

At 3.30pm we leave Sint-Idesbald. Hendrik is in the passenger seat. Tom, his right-hand man, at the wheel. In the back are Thomas, the photographer, and myself, the author. The plan is for me to write *on the road.* I've travelled quite a bit over the past years, but this is my first time in a camper van and it's a revelation. As it is for Tom, Hendrik and Thomas too. Our road trip itinerary has us arriving in Paris at the restaurant A Table in four hours, then continuing to Rungis in the night. From there on to the Corrèze, followed by the Pyrénées and Biarritz. On the agenda: meetings and discussions with livestock farmers. The shelves and fridges of the van are well stocked. *Côte à l'os,* sausages, pâtés, aged entrecôtes, ham, *cervelat,* brawn, black and white tripe, rillettes, bacon, everything you could dream of. We've even brought a small lamb on board, which I hear Hendrik plans to prepare in the mountains. The space next to the sink is filled with bread, mustard, pickles, salads, bell peppers and lots of fruit. There's also beer and several crates of wine… We have water. We will certainly not die of hunger or thirst. Hendrik is going to cook. Thomas is going to take pictures. I'm going to write. Tom is driving. Tom is also our DJ. Our trip begins to the sound of the Pixies playing 'Here Comes Your Man'.

RUNGIS

PARIS

Tuesday 5pm – On the road

Lille, traffic jams. The landscape of northern France rolls by. The flowers of early May. Wheat and mustard fields, vast plains. Arras passes on our right. Johnny Cash's 'Jackson' plays in the background.

Hendrik says: "I want to make a book that tells the story of an evolving profession. The butcher was once an important figure in the neighbourhood, in his village. Many butchers have disappeared because the soul of the profession has become somewhat lost along the way. I don't know if you can speak of a revival now, but something's happening, with the rise of new-style butchers in the United States and England, and a handful of certified butchers in France. And something is also happening among the people, as awareness is growing that it is important and necessary to eat less meat – as you can see in the increasing number of vegans and vegetarians, for whom I have respect – and in the 'nose-to-tail' movement, a way of treating the animal that I have a keen interest in. I've wanted to become a butcher since I was a child. I want to practice this profession the way my father did, with my hands in the meat and my feet in the grasslands, but I want to respond to modern expectations and make use of the new opportunities of our time.

"We have knowledge at our disposal that previous generations did not. Anyone who loves the butcher's trade today needs to be present in their shop, of course, but also in their atelier, at the market, in the slaughterhouse, with the sellers, with the breeders… You have to be familiar with the herds, the breeds, the terroirs, and you have to share that knowledge with your customers. You can learn a lot from meeting people. You get to know the characteristic world of the livestock farmers, you meet dealers and restaurateurs. David Martin from La Paix restaurant was the first to have faith in me, and he encouraged me to believe in what I was doing. Through Sergio Herman I discovered guts and creativity: the idea that the sky's the limit. Kobe Desramaults has also been very important to me. Kobe heightened my awareness of the importance of terroir, of respect for life. But there are more. I learn something from people every day. That's the story that I would like to tell you, without forgetting the basics, of course, because it is that basis, the traditional element of the butcher's craft, that inspired me to be a butcher. There! I wanted to say that!"

Silence. 'Rocket Queen' by Guns N' Roses plays softly. A sign flits by the car window: Paris 180 km.

Tuesday 7pm

Black Sabbath. 'Iron Man'.

We revisit what Hendrik said about his father. That he was an old-school butcher, the embodiment of the traditional butcher's trade. It's in his blood. He's retired and could be taking it easy, but he still comes into the shop every day. He barely went to school and learned the craft with a butcher in the village, then with other butchers, in Antwerp and Brussels. He wanted to be able to do everything. Selecting a beautiful animal, carving it up, discussing with the customers, making his own pâtés and tripes. Loving what you do and being proud of it. "My father is old school. And I am also old school. And Tom here is old school too."

Tom gets up, cuts the dry sausage, slices the bread. He prepares the mustard and cracks open three bottles of beer.

Another 90 kilometres to Paris, a sign says.

8pm. Blue sky. First beers. Grant Lee Buffalo.'Fuzzy'.

Wednesday 3.30am – Rungis parking lot

It's night. The van is standing in the parking lot of the meat hall. The alarm goes off. We've slept for two hours. The air is brisk. We splash some water on our faces and brush our teeth. It's actually quite chilly. Waning moon. Trucks coming and going. Doors slamming. We are in Rungis, the largest fresh produce market in the world. More than 12,000 people work here; 25,000 customers arrive every night. There are butchers, cheesemongers, fishmongers, poulterers, *affineurs,* the curious, cooks and sellers, all crowding around these exceptional products. Hendrik gets out of the car. He's wearing an immaculately clean white apron and a logo-bearing cap, the mandatory dress code. He gives us capes and plastic caps to wear. We look a bit silly.

Laughing all around.

EURODIS

Wednesday 4am – Coffee at the Saint-Hubert bistro

We have a *café crème* with croissants and pastries at the Saint-Hubert, a brasserie in the meat hall. Nowhere in France are more cups of coffee consumed in a day than here: 2,500 that is, from the middle of the night to the early morning. Caricature sketches of former meat sellers up on the walls. Talking and laughing around us. And sometimes a glass of Loire white wine is raised to seal a sale. Picturesque atmosphere and buzzing crowds. A city within a city, where Hendrik appears to know quite a lot of people. We promise to visit one, and another, and a third.

Rungis opened its doors on 27 February 1969, a few months before humans first set foot on the moon. The famous halls – christened *le ventre de Paris,* the belly of Paris, by Emile Zola – moved here in five days. 30,000 people all at once. 1,000 producers; 10,000 cubic metres of material; 5,000 tons of merchandise and 5,000 trucks… The French government briefly considered deploying the army, but in the end each merchant chose to take care of his own relocation. The flowers kicked off the move on Thursday; the next day it was the turn of fruit and vegetables; then dairy followed: butter, cheese and eggs. Meat and sea produce closed the line on 1 March. A tour de force! But with the departure of the market that Louis VI had installed in the heart of the city in the first half of the 12th century, Paris also lost a part of its soul.

Hendrik: "I came here for the first time about sixteen years ago, with my father and a few colleagues. We were looking for something new. In Belgium at that time, the Belgian Blue breed was the most well known. There was also Maine-Anjou and Holstein cattle, but they were mainly used for milk and for breeding. Some butchers had their own cattle, like we had our West Flemish Red, but that wasn't enough. Then British Angus beef made its appearance. After the crisis of the 1990s, the British were building up a new and interesting herd. I had also met a few farmers in the Corrèze. Transportation was not easy. We were also doing some renovations in the shop during that period. My father, my mother and Evelyne, we always paid a lot of attention to the shop window, to keeping it neat, tidy and varied. Beef on one side, lamb, pork, chicken and duck on the other. We wanted to show our customers everything out in the open, but it had to look good. For all these reasons we went to Rungis.

And we loved it. The meat you can discover there… Maybe all animals are not equally beautiful, but what a diversity! Veal calves. Salt-marsh lambs. Simmental. Aubrac. Salers. Blonde d'Aquitaine. All those breeds… It made a big impression on us. And the poultry… Incredible capons. Bresse chickens. Black grouse from Britain. Pigeons. Hares. Bellotta hams. Ibérico. Pigs… It was beautiful. You couldn't find anything like that in Belgium. And then there was La Triperie. An entire pavilion. Pig heads that were carved up. Kilos of kidneys. It was an impressive sight to take in. We walked around there all night and, later, I often went back alone. I would observe the people and watch them work. I learned to understand and appreciate the art of animal selection. One specialised in Simmental, another in Salers or Aubrac, a third in milk-fed calves. I discovered new breeds: Aberdeen Angus, Rubia Gallega, Wagyu, Kobe… I learned how to buy. You don't cheat in this environment. You pay and you receive. And that worked. I became familiar with those people. And my client base grew. I have invested a lot into this, both time and money. Gaining someone's trust takes time. A market like this is a special place. There are codes. Not all products look good. Most of it is middle of the road, but what is beautiful is sometimes exceptionally beautiful. It took two to three years before I was accepted. But when that time comes, you are considered part of the family."

Wednesday 4.40am – Rungis. Meat hall

Many hundreds of slaughtered animals, hanging on a hook. The placards state the breed and origin: Aubrac, Salers, Irish Angus, Normandy… A little further down we find Charolais, Blonde d'Aquitaine and Blonde de Galice. Some animals have been awarded prizes at a market. A seller tells us that he has never regretted specialising in the import of German beef. "Twenty years ago, you only found French meat. But times and customs are changing. Simmental is a Bavarian variety. Beautiful, naturally marbled meat. Animals weighing 400 to 500 kilos, a lot of meat on them, nicely layered with fat and full loins." Another explains to us that the presence of fat on the slaughtered animal guarantees beautifully marbled meat.

Hendrik confirms this: he has a few regular suppliers. All he has to do is make a phone call and explain what he's looking for, and they'll find the carcass or rack he wants. He goes to Rungis once or twice a month. Between November and New Year he has to go a few times a week, because the demand for quality products is that high then. But Rungis has changed. You will still find good products there, but the market has become a conduit for products from just about everywhere. The situation changed with the opening of borders and the liberalisation of trade. Incidentally, after the discovery of Rungis market, Hendrik also started researching breeders and slaughterhouses. He now buys some of his animals directly from farmers in France, Italy, Spain or Ireland. The slaughtered animals are shipped to Rungis, where the butcher has the use of cooling rooms. From there he transports them to Belgium. Some of the purchasing is still done through the Rungis sellers. Butchers can buy carved pieces of meat at the wholesale market. But loyalty and confidence remain essential. A dealer explains: "You must understand, every now and then we get a visit from a Belgian butcher who is looking for beautiful meat. We listen to him, but before we say yes or no, we advise him to visit Hendrik. That is simpler."

A seller: "Hendrik. This here…" Hendrik looks and walks over to another carcass. The seller calls him back: "Not enough fat for you? How about this one here?" The seller presses his finger on the fine layer of fat on the back of an animal next to it. Milk-fed calf from the Corrèze. The butcher looks, touches, presses and selects… "You can put this aside for me. And this one too…" The seller takes notes. Prices are not discussed. The trust seems mutual. In the back a dozen men are at work, sliding the carcasses along the rails. A ballet, a handful of words, and the sound of the axe cutting the carcasses lengthwise.

The seller says: "Veal is a delicate meat. You can't cut it with an electric saw. You'd burn the bone and marrow, and the meat would take on some of the burnt smell. You have to cut the calf with an axe. The men who do that are Malians."

"Malians?"

The seller: "Yes. Many Malians work in the meat hall at Rungis. This has been the case for several years. A bit of a coincidence at first, but then some families developed a specialisation in that work. Strong, fast men. Guys you can trust, always on time for work. The skill to split a slaughtered animal in half, from top to bottom, either you have it or you don't… I can see it immediately. And the Malians have that knack. For them, it seems like child's play. They are strong and they work very precisely. Calmly, without forcing. They can split 100 carcasses in one night."

Hendrik takes a look and confirms the purchase.

I ask him what makes the difference. "The colour and the fat. Veal should not have too much fat, but it does need a little. On the back. If there is fat on the underside of the neck and body, then you know you'll get beautifully marbled meat."

Me: "And this here?"

Hendrik: "A bit heavy… Too fat… Too thick flanks for me. I know my clientele. My customers won't buy meat that is too fatty."

The seller moves a few metres further: "Check this out…"

Hendrik: "Too dark in colour!" The seller anticipates my question and explains that people want light veal. They want white meat. But that is not easy. Now they want light meat with fat.

And Hendrik explains: "That implies that the calf drank only milk. A milk-fed calf has never eaten grass. As soon as a calf eats grass, the flesh changes colour. I'll explain it to you in the Corrèze…"

"YOU DON'T CHEAT IN THIS ENVIRONMENT. YOU PAY AND YOU RECEIVE. AND THAT WORKED. I BECAME FAMILIAR WITH THOSE PEOPLE."

Wednesday 5am – Rungis
'Paris s'éveille.' Café de l'Europe. Steak au poivre

Hendrik and I order steak au poivre, Tom an entrecôte. It's five in the morning and the day is dawning, but we're eating steak and drinking a couple of beers as if that's normal. A seller is still sitting with us. There is talk about the stagnant prices, about the trade, and about how difficult it is to find rare gems. Consumers are becoming increasingly choosy and always want better merchandise without wanting to pay the price. The seller explains how much everything has changed in the past 20 years. A good seller has contacts with the slaughterhouses. He tells them what his customers want. And in the slaughterhouse, the message is conveyed to the farmers. To each their own profession. In this way, the suppliers almost become partners. Requirements vary according to the season. The most important step forward in the last 20 years has been traceability. Each animal has labels, stamps, an identity card; every step of its trajectory is known, from the pasture to the plate. A seller knows where the animal comes from, how it was fed and who fed it. This information is passed on to the butcher, who in turn can pass it on to his customers. "We cut according to the orders: more or less fat, thicker or less thick… The art of meat cutting is a whole other story."

9.15am, on the road to Corrèze. Time for a siesta. In the background Dylan sings 'Just like a Woman'.

CORRÈZE

MILK-FED CALVES

Wednesday 2pm – Corrèze

Roy Orbison, 'I Drove All Night'. Just before Brive we take the off-ramp to Tulle. A beautiful, undulating road that follows the river and meanders around the hills towards the Massif Central. France can be so beautiful! The famous orange and red Limousin cattle graze in the fields. The landscape is green. The forests, the grasslands, the air, everything is singing spring. We drive to Saint-Chamant and then on to Argentat, on the banks of the Dordogne, where Limousin, Auvergne and Quercy meet. This is the region of truffles and milk-fed calves, a livestock with centuries of tradition. Just think of the worship of the golden calf in the Old Testament and the other biblical story of the fatted calf that was slaughtered to celebrate the return of the prodigal son.

After the Second World War, this delightful tradition suffered from the development of intensive livestock farming focused on increasing production. Out of laziness and for 36 other wrong reasons, farmers began to raise calves on an industrial scale just about everywhere, replacing mother's milk with powdered milk and other additives. Three to four weeks after birth, the calves are separated from their mothers and then fattened up in specialised ateliers for four to five months. Everything is geared towards quantity, and that comes at the expense of quality. Because this way of working was financially interesting, quite a few farmers at the time decided to abandon traditional farming practices.

In the Corrèze, some opponents of the new approach then united to defend their interests, convinced as they were of the value of the traditional practices, which were perfectly suited to their region. The first Red Label (Label Rouge), *Veau sous la mère,* was created in 1971. In the 1980s, other regional labels followed suit, aiming for control of the breeding process and optimum quality. They were combined in 2011 under the label *Veau fermier élevé sous la mère.*

"LIVESTOCK FARMERS DO EVERYTHING TO BREED THE BEST ANIMALS. IT'S THEIR LIFE. IT'S THEIR PRIDE."

Consumers like veal that is white to light pink, but also marbled, a sign of quality. That is the case with a calf that is exclusively fed with milk. Milk is low in iron and requires the young animal to use its own reserves to grow. The depletion of those reserves results in the pale colour of the muscles. In the Corrèze, calves have been fed exclusively with the milk of their mother for decades, complemented by that of 'nursing cows', the so-called aunts.

Wednesday, late afternoon – La Guinguette du Malpas

Cattle dealer Jean-Yves Martinigol joins us at our table. He works for the Argentat slaughterhouse, which specialises in calves. He knows the breeders of the region, visits them on the farms and keeps track of how the herds evolve. Most farmers work only with this slaughterhouse. Sometimes they keep a few animals for livestock markets, where they occasionally win prizes. This region hosts some of the most beautiful cattle markets in France, such as those of Brive-la-Gaillarde, Objat, Saint-Robert, Beaulieu-sur-Dordogne, Meyssac, Maurs, Saint-Constant and Saint-Céré.

Jean-Yves: "In the 1970s, a number of breeders joined forces and created the first Red Label. They were visionary. Quality was the most important thing for them. Their approach, with controls and traceability, was reassuring for the consumer market. Consumers were also starting to show concern about the living conditions of calves in industrial livestock farming. And then there were the scandals with the hormones. Because of those kinds of things the traditional farmers have managed to survive. Those who have opted for this approach have no regrets, even though it is a very demanding form of livestock farming.

"Everything is done to make sure the meat is as pale as possible. For one thing calves are not allowed any food other than milk. So they are never allowed to go outside. In the past, farmers used to put muzzles on the animals to prevent them from eating anything else in the barn, such as hay.

And it was always very dark in there, so the animals stayed calm. The calves were kept in tiny individual pens, sometimes attached to their mother with one leg. New animal welfare legislation has forced farmers to revise their way of working. Individual cages and muzzles are now things of the past, but that was not always welcomed by the traditional farmers, who saw their income fall as a result of this reform. The new generation is more attentive to the welfare of the animals, which, by the way, also guarantees good health and better quality. Even if the meat might then be a little less white…

"Buying and selling is easy. But finding a quality product that meets the requirements of buyers is another matter. Everyone wants flavoursome meat, but who is willing to pay the price for it? When you know what it takes to produce quality meat, the price being asked is correct. You should know what a farmer has to do for it. Every day, they get up early in the morning and they don't go to bed until late at night… I like to spend time with them. I spend my days on the farms, outdoors at all hours. I love talking with them, exchanging stories. A farmer does have a tendency to always complain, argue, criticise… but he'll stop that once you've earned his trust. Livestock farmers do everything they can to breed the best animals. It's their life. It is their pride. And the result of their work is worth it. Our calves have never been more beautiful than they are today. In the Corrèze, the farmers love what they do."

SÉBASTIEN SOURSAC

Breeder of milk-fed calves – Le Chassaing, Sioniac

"I learned the business of farming from my grandfather. The farmers were champions of a way of working that was perfect for the region. Our farms are small, 30 or 40 hectares: agriculture on a human scale. In addition to breeding our animals, we also do a bit of agriculture. Some farmers have plums, I have strawberries. Strawberries have become so easy. If we had to start all over, we probably wouldn't grow anything but strawberries. I love my animals, let there be no doubt about that. But if you want nice white veal, you have to be there all the time, that's the problem. As soon as the weather is nice, we put the cows in the meadow. We have wonderfully clean and nutrient-rich grass. The animals benefit from this all summer long. In the winter they stay in the barn, nursing the calves. That's not difficult to monitor, but it takes a lot of time. New systems have been devised to facilitate suckling, with the mothers taking care of things themselves. At my farm, the calf goes to its mother. In other places, it is sometimes done the other way around and it is the cow that goes to her calf. The calves drink once in the morning and once in the afternoon, always at fixed times. The more they drink from their mother, the better. And we, we keep an eye on everything. During the first month, a calf drinks only its mother's milk. Limousin cows give very nutritious milk, but not in great quantities. A mother can generally nurse her young up to about 100 kilos. Afterwards it is a bit of a struggle to get to 140, 150 kilos. We also need to grow some fat on them. The meat must be white, but also contain enough fat. It's quite an art. To make up for the shortage of milk in the Limousin cows, most farmers have a few extra cows, often Normande or Montbeliarde cattle, good dairy cows that can suckle the calves. We call them the 'aunties'."

JEAN-LOUIS, RÉMY & VINCENT ARRESTIER

Father and sons, breeders of milk-fed calves – Le Mons, Monceaux-sur-Dordogne

"We have about 50 cows. Every year there are about 40 calves. We raise them here for four and a half months, sometimes five months. A calf weighs between 140 and 160 kilos when it's sent to the slaughterhouse. That is the normal way to do it. But a white calf is always an adventure. My father started in 1996. The first BSE crisis took place during that period. It was a tragedy everywhere, except for the milk-fed calves. Not a single case! And that's no coincidence. Farmers who invest in beautiful and solid work have no complaints. We make a living from this. We don't grumble, we love what we do, but it's hard work. There are three of us, my father, my brother Vincent and myself, and that's why we can give each other a break now and then. We can also rely on our family. It would be difficult without family. In the winter it's easy, then the animals are inside. Then we have control. And we give them our own hay. We know what the animals are eating. We prefer the cold, harsh winters: then the animals stay indoors for a long time. The later the beautiful days come, the better. The cows go outside in the spring. Then they eat grass and then we have no more control, because the milk changes. And when the milk changes, everything changes: the flavour and the colour, of both the butter and the veal. A calf only comes out of the barn to go to the slaughterhouse. It is now the beginning of May and the last calf left two days ago. Some farmers keep one or two to raise as future mothers. But that's a delicate undertaking. You have to raise them for three years before they calve for the first time. That costs money and you can never be sure of a good return. My father and I prefer to buy nice heifers from other farmers. They become the future mothers. After seven or eight years, when they are no longer in calf, the old ones go to the slaughterhouse as beef cows."

PYRÉNÉES

FR
453 855
80019

MILK-FED LAMBS

Friday 9am – To the Pyrénées

Coffee with croissants and chocolate buns at the Argentat slaughterhouse. Director Miquel Yorick gives us a tour and explains how important it is that a cow is transported to the slaughterhouse in the best possible conditions. When an animal is slaughtered under stressful conditions it diminishes the quality of the meat. The last hours are crucial. The departure from the farm, the loading, the transport, the wait in the anaesthesia department, all must be arranged with the utmost care. For example, denying food, which was customary in the past, intensifies the animal's reaction. But the stress is also exacerbated by the isolation, the rough treatment, the shouting…

After the visit we drive south, heading for the Pyrénées. A two-hour trip over the roads of Quercy. We meet two pilgrims on their way to Compostela. The landscape is fabulous. Along the Dordogne, with Beaulieu and then Saint-Céré. Rising and falling, rising and falling… Meadows, fields, forests. On the way to Gramat, a herd of Saler cattle with long horns reminds us that the mountains of Cantal and Auvergne are not far from here. Beautiful beasts with red skin. Then more fields, meadows and forests, and then the limestone terraces that herald the wine of Cahors, and Lalbenque, the heartlands of the black truffle. And then on to the highway.

Music. Black Keys. 'Gold on the Ceiling'.

"CELEBRITY CHEFS HAVE PUT OUR PRODUCTS ON THEIR MENU."

Saturday afternoon, at the table of Mrs Burguburu – Sainte-Engrâce

The landscape that surrounds us this afternoon is truly without equal. To the right we see the Romanesque church of Sainte-Engrâce, one of the oldest religious buildings in the Basque Country. By the small cemetery, some hikers are taking a breather before starting their journey to the forest of Iraty and the gorges of Kakuetta and Ehujarre, which, we are told, are extremely beautiful. In the distance we can see the mountain peaks of the Igountze and the Legorre. This is historically a region of shepherds, smugglers, resistance fighters; in short, of people who know what they want. The people here are proud to be Basque. They look you in the eye and greet you with a firm handshake. Jean-Jacques takes us to Auberge Elixaltea, where a welcoming and copious meal awaits us. Only local products are featured on the menu of Mrs Burguburu: piperade (omelette with tomato and bell pepper), Basque chicken, goat's cheese and home-made pie. Delicious.

JEAN-JACQUES SALLABERREMBORDE

Director of the Axuria cooperative, known for its Pyrenean milk-fed lambs

"The Axuria cooperative was founded in 1983 by a dozen livestock farmers who wanted to leave the traditional path and gain more control over the commercialisation of the milk-fed lamb. We started slaughtering lambs in this region to protect the more profitable cheese industry; so the lambs wouldn't drink all the fresh milk the sheep produce. Lamb meat wasn't as interesting then. Most of the animals were exported alive to Italy. That was not very profitable. Still, we had good-quality lambs. The pioneers focused their attention on this, and with success. In the beginning, the cooperative sent 2,000 lambs a year to the Mauléon slaughterhouse; now it has 250 members and supplies 50,000 lambs a year… But we are still able to work on a human scale, with respect for the traditional way of farming. Our lamb comes from strong local breeds: Basco-béarnaise, Manech tête noire and Manech tête rousse. We know we can't compete with the British or New Zealand lamb. Our lambs are more expensive, but better… We have received a Red Label and an AOP *(Appellation d'Origine Protégée)*. Our ex-chairman, Michel Arhancet, has also reached out to celebrity chefs, who have become our partners and ambassadors – Yves Camdeborde, for example, and Christian Constant, in particular, the former chef of Crillon restaurant in Paris. They have supported us by putting our products on their menus. Other chefs have followed. Everything happens on a human scale, I cannot emphasise that enough. All of our farmers are located close to the cooperative. For several years now, we have also been selling cattle, both cows and calves, especially Blonde d'Aquitaine and Limousin cattle. They are beautiful dairy cows and calves, fed with their mother's milk, supplemented with cereals. It's quite successful. They are slaughtered at six months. We work with 300 farmers. I am very satisfied with our lambs, which have now acquired a certain fame, but our beef farming can still be improved on. We still have to work on our mentality. Sometimes a particularly beautiful animal weighing 500 kilos is better than a rather mediocre animal weighing 600 kilos. That striving for quality should be present in everything. Taking the time to fatten them up with grass. Never forcing anything. The muscle must be given time to be layered with fat. There used to be a great variety of breeds in the Pyrénées. We could consider working with the Blonde des Pyrénées, for example. If you want to deliver quality, you have to distinguish yourself from the rest and focus on your own terroirs."

PEIO QUIHILLALT

Breeder of milk-fed lamb
Saturday afternoon – Athérey

"The family businesses here are quite small. Two hundred sheep, about 50 cows. We have to adapt to local circumstances. The Basque Country is a region of mountains and valleys. The *transhumance* (seasonal migration between pastures) makes the difference. In autumn, winter and spring, our sheep are in the valley or in the barn. In summer, we go into the mountains. Then we go with the sheep and the cows to the high meadows, because it becomes too dry in the valleys. The empty fields are used to farm hay to feed the animals in the winter. In the past, a shepherd stayed up in the mountains for a few months. Now the circumstances are such that he can have a better family life. We divvy up the time in the mountains among eight shepherds. I like to be there. I stay for three days. I love the bleakness. Time to think, dream, breathe. Being alone with the sheep and the dogs. We call that the *estive*. The frost has passed by early June, but the peaks are still snowy. As the ground turns green and the snow melts, we climb higher and higher, as high as 1,700–1,800 metres. The sheep are filled with new energy and lots of vitamins to feed their little ones during winter. We will come down again in September. The sheep are in lamb by then. Most lambs are born between November and May. When they're born, we have to make sure they drink well. They drink nothing but milk from their mother. They are slaughtered after four to six weeks. They then weigh between nine and 11 kilos, carcass weight. The flesh is pinkish-white and has a very delicate flavour. In this way we make maximum use of our terroir. And we don't let anything go to waste. We use the milk to make cheese: an AOP-labelled Ossau-Iraty, and a local brocciu, which is made from the whey that some farmers give to the pigs. Pearls before swine..."

Saturday evening, night in the Pyrénées

Around 6pm, Hendrik takes the wheel of the camper van. We follow lamb farmer Peio and drive to the mountain top over a dirt road. We stop there. Down in the valley you can see Licq-Athérey. A few cows, a herd of goats, the red roofs of the farms and the green of the pastures. The last snow on the mountain tops is slowly vanishing beneath the sun of these first fine days. Tom takes out the folding chairs and Hendrik uncorks a bottle. Time for a barbecue. On the menu: milk-fed lamb with a tomato salad. The sun sets and the night falls.

We look at the stars. Without music. Only wind. Lots of wind.

STEENVOORDE

'PIGEONNEAU DE M. DEQUIDT'

ALEX DEQUIDT

Tuesday morning, pigeon breeder – Steenvoorde

Even though we're in France, the landscape looks decidedly Flemish. Poperinge (Belgium) is just a few kilometres away. A strong wind is blowing over the sun-drenched countryside. Alex Dequidt has been breeding pigeons for more than 30 years. It's a family business; his two sons have also been working here for the last dozen or so years. Because of their passion for their trade and their expertise, they're highly thought of by the best restaurants in the region. Alex and Hendrik have been working together for more than ten years.

Alex: "I'm a farmer's son. I started out working in restaurants. Some great places: Le Flambard, Queen Victoria… However, after ten years, I was longing for the country again. At that time, now more than 30 years ago, you could sense the agricultural departments were pushing to help farming companies diversify their activities. I could have opted for rabbit or some other fowl, but we chose pigeons. A bit of a coincidence, actually. There are quite a few pigeon fanciers in the mining area, but for them it is primarily a hobby and a sport. They breed their pigeons to participate in competitions. And because not all pigeons in their loft can be champions, the lesser gods go into the pan.

"It wasn't easy in the beginning. There are plenty who tried but were unsuccessful, because breeding pigeons requires a special kind of focus. Heavy investments are not necessary, but you have to be present. I started small, with 64 pairs. You just have to put them all together. The first one chooses the prettiest female, the last takes what's left… The male lures the female into a nest that the pair then keeps for life, four and a half years. When the female has laid an egg, the male incubates it. We work according to traditional methods. Pigeon farming is extensive. The lofts are open and exposed to the wind. I don't interfere in any way. We feed the parents, but they feed their young with a thick goop that they regurgitate from their crop. It's the same in winter and summer.

"I started small and learned along the way. We all have our little secrets. Sometimes we run out of birds and can't deliver. Then we'll ask a colleague to help us out of the emergency. Afterwards you sometimes hear the customer say: 'I don't know, but that pigeon last time was not the same…' The Belgians are especially demanding. They are real connoisseurs. In some restaurants, the menu announces *Pigeonneau de M. Dequidt* – and we are quite proud of that. Or when a housewife on the market says: 'Your pigeons are really extraordinary, I can't say anything else, extraordinary…', that gives me real pleasure. It is a privilege for us to be able to do what we do.

"I don't want to give too much away, but the key word is homogeneity. We take the squabs out of the nest to slaughter when feathers start appearing under the wings. They all have about the same weight and physique. This is important. The chef of the restaurant, or the housewife, then has identical squabs in terms of the texture and colour of the meat. The pigeons that the pigeon fanciers supplied used to all look alike, but were different ages. With a delicate meat like this, you can't afford that. You have to work precisely and carefully.

"We produce around 1,000 squabs per week. We are fortunate to have our own slaughterhouse. In this way, we can supply the finished product: pigeons that have been slaughtered according to traditional methods, and dry-plumed with wax. Everything is done manually. We put the pigeons in a bath of wax, then put them in cold water and remove the wax, like peeling an egg. Dead simple. We are pioneers. We have experimented with things and found out new ways. That makes our pigeons different."

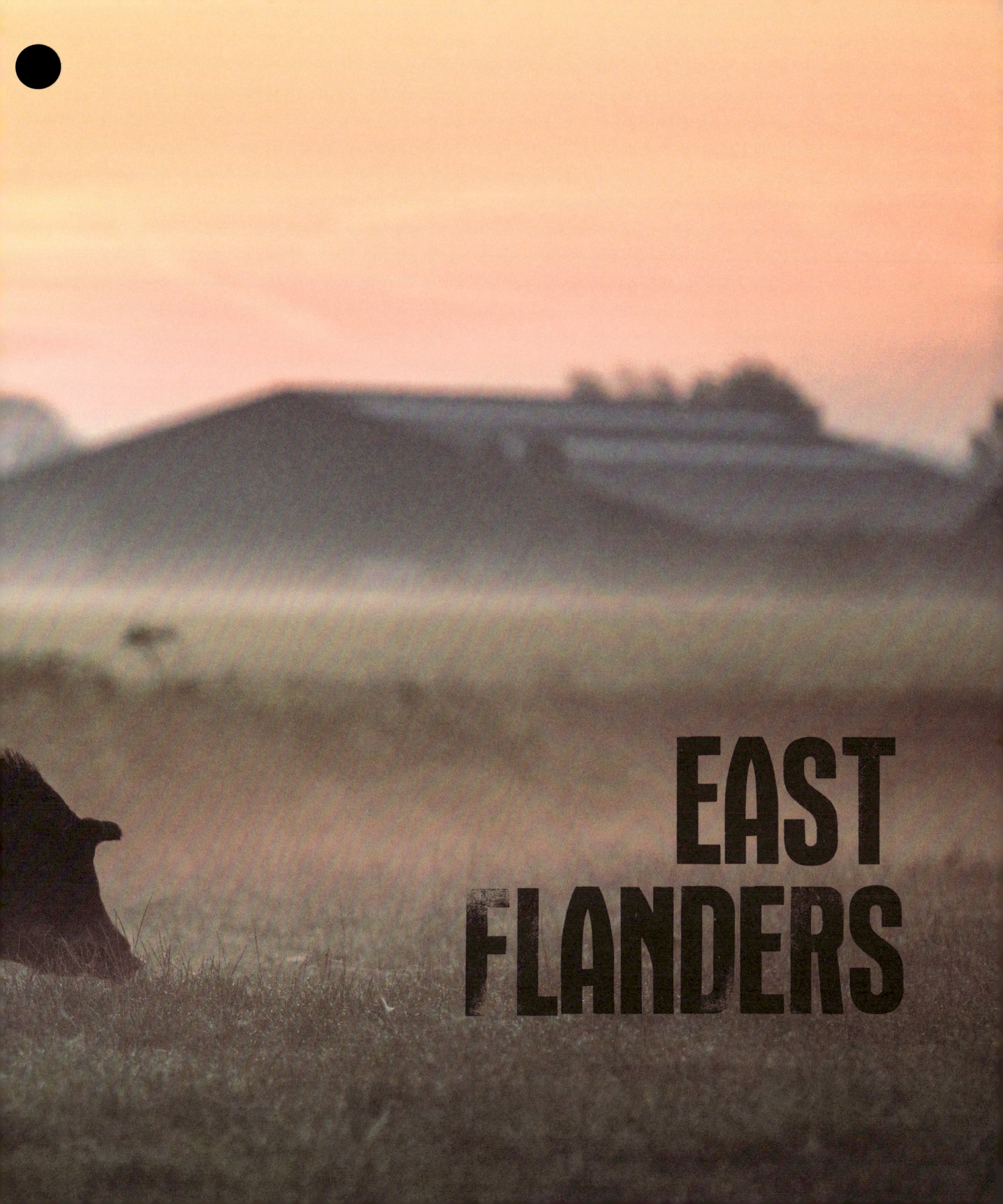

EAST FLANDERS

THE MENAPIAN PIG

RUBEN BRABANT

Wednesday, pig breeder – Nevele, East Flanders

"When you love what you do 100 percent and are very passionate and proud of your profession, then you're always on the lookout for something different, something better, something innovative. It may seem strange that you have to look to the very distant past for this, as a butcher or a breeder, and yet that is the reality. You need to take a step back, reset, to rebuild something. That was the idea behind our adventure with the Menapian pig. A quest to find the Flemish primeval pig. This journey started five years ago, with the help of the pig breeder Ruben Brabant, one of those amazing chance encounters in life. We both happened to be looking for the same elusive thing, which is why we decided to join forces.

"A shared acquaintance then pointed us in the direction of Ghent University, where Professor Benedikt Sas and archaeologist Wim De Clercq were interested in what we had to say. They helped the last piece of the puzzle to finally fall into place. Wim had recently excavated the bones of a pig that roamed our land 2,000 years ago near the coast. Usually, bones are never preserved for that long in acidic soil but this was an exception, because of the naturally occurring lime and historic use of loam as a building material. It's always nice when you have a break. Further research revealed that these were the bones of a half-wild, half-domesticated pig, which they found in the forest and which was prized during the Roman Empire for its meat. Many old texts literally refer to the Menapian pig. Ruben and I had finally found our Holy Grail.

"The name is derived from the Menapians, a peasant tribe that lived around 50 BC in northern Gaul, in the region that is known today as West Flanders, East Flanders and Zeeland Flanders. The tribe's speciality? Breeding pigs, of course. In those days, they used to brine and dry meat to preserve it, meaning it could be kept for long periods of time. And the Romans loved it. They even supplied it to their legions on their long and arduous tours of duty. Flanders' oldest official export product, in other words.

"Now all we had to do was bring this almost mythical Menapian pig back to life. Easier said than done. To all intents and purposes, the process was not in any way like the method used in Steven Spielberg's blockbuster *Jurassic Park* from the early 1990s. We could only extract DNA from the bones for a comparative study. Currently, we are almost there. But first Ruben had to identify the best possible cross-breeds from which to breed a Menapian pig, or something that resembled it very closely. Without wishing to reveal all his secrets, I can disclose that this process involved a real boar and a few ancient pig breeds.

"In the meantime, Menapian pigs have been walking in and around his stable in Nevele for a few years now. One of the most noticeable things about them is their dark, woolly coat. They also have a crest on their back, which they can raise to look more imposing. Although they're slightly smaller than ordinary pigs, they make up for the difference in size with their temperament. A moment of inattention, and they will have ripped your skin with their impressive tusks. They are wild animals, after all.

"CUTLETS OF MENAPIAN PIGS CAN LAST FOR UP TO TEN DAYS, ENHANCING AND ADDING POWER TO THE FLAVOUR. REALLY MAGNIFICENT."

And 'survival of the fittest' is a way of life for them. The weakest piglets are sometimes eaten, without mercy, by their mothers. They are also very curious and have a strong herd instinct. If one is stubborn, the others will follow suit.

"Our Menapian pigs spend almost all their time – 12 to 14 months depending on our plans for them – outside, are very resilient and are not given antibiotics. Pigs used for charcuterie spend more time outside because that's the only way to obtain excellent lardo-like back bacon and big hams with plenty of fat. The first animals we slaughtered revealed that the meat is not as pale as that of an average pig. It is pinkish to dark red, with a very fine texture. Like boar, it also has a very fine grain. And because of cross-breeding, there is some marbling. The best of both worlds, in fact. The meat is also very dense, not too tender. I have pork that has been aging for three weeks here. You would never have been able to do this in the past. Cutlets of Menapian pigs can last for up to ten days, enhancing and adding power to the flavour. Really magnificent. And you can taste a certain wildness in the fat. Exactly what Ruben and I had in mind.

"All we have to do now is fine-tune their food. Some employees of Ghent University are currently re-examining old texts to find out what these creatures would have been fed in the past, which wild herbs they would have foraged for, and so on. We have already come so far, much further than we ever dared hope, but I'm sure the Menapian pig has plenty of other developments in store for us."

BACHTEN DE KUPE

OUR WEST FLEMISH RED BEEF

RAYMOND DIERENDONCK

Thursday. Butcher, *charcutier* and breeder of West Flemish Red cows – Sint-Idesbald

6pm. Tom stops the car and turns off the music. The end of the journey, the beginning of the story. We're parked at the family farm, a few kilometres from Sint-Idesbald. I'd already spent a day there a few weeks earlier, when Hendrik explained his plans for a book to me. It was in the afternoon. The table was set with white sausages and black pudding, home-made pâté, ham, pastrami and farmhouse bread. A beautiful spread. And, of course, the wine flowed freely… Hendrik started talking about the place where he grew up. About his parents, about his childhood, about the butcher shop. That's where everything started. We talked about books and about music. He got up and played *Frank's Wild Years* by Tom Waits. It was a February afternoon. The weather was nice. He also told me about that Tom Waits concert, in Ghent or in Paris, I don't remember. Then we talked about the book again. He told me what he would like. "Something simple, but something real," he said. "Something that is simple, yet strong… Just tell our story. First the story of my father and mother. Start with what they created and then continue with what I've done, with what we've built together."

Raymond comes out and welcomes us. He starts telling the tale: "After we got married, we wanted to set up our own business. Sint-Idesbald, a small tourist village between De Panne and Koksijde, seemed like a good place to establish ourselves. We started small, in 1970. Those were different times. There were six butchers in the village then, now there are two. And of the three fishmongers, two are left. The first years we worked hard in the busy months of July and August. Later on, the tourist season became a bit longer. First, weekend tourists in May, June and September. Then all year round. But in the early years there wasn't much work in the butcher's shop during the winter. The local people would leave for a few months to work in the sugar factory in Veurne. And because I loved animals, I decided to start raising them myself.

"After a few years I had about 30 cows, a few chickens and several pastures. I worked independently and my animals brought extra income to the butcher's shop. They were Maine-Anjou cattle, a French breed from the Loire region; excellent cattle for dairy and beef. I loved those robust, quirky, handsome beasts. I sold the calves on for fattening and kept the best cows. Every now and then, I bought a few animals to infuse the herd with new blood. I had never been a fan of the Belgian Blue breed. It's easy to say that today, but 25 years ago everyone was raving about it. And I had to explain my choice to my clients. Blue cattle may well yield tender meat, but I think it lacks flavour. Maine-Anjou produces nicely marbled, red and juicy flesh. The taste comes from the fat. And you get a nice fat when you combine this breed with a livestock breeder who knows what he's doing, and a good diet. Also, the animal needs to live outside. My animals grazed here, in the polders. The grass here is excellent. The sea breeze, the salt in the environment, it all contributes to the quality and taste. And we were in no hurry. We took our time to fatten up the animals.

"We had to find a way to explain all our choices to our customers. So they could understand. What determines the taste? Why is fat so important? How do you cook a *côte à l'os?* Why do you have to take the meat out of the fridge two hours before cooking? Why do you have to let the meat rest before cutting it? When do you use butter? Or olive oil?

"WEST FLEMISH RED BEEF IS NATIVE TO THIS REGION AND IS ABLE TO MAKE THE MOST OF THE QUALITIES TYPICAL OF WESTHOEK'S ECOSYSTEM."

By taking the time to tell our customers all about these things, we have taught them to appreciate the fat. We did things a different way. We didn't make black pudding just to be different, we made 'our' black pudding, 'our' pâté. I'm not saying it's better than any other butcher's, but it tastes the way we like it.

"We have expanded the business and developed a catering service offering meatballs, vol-au-vent, spaghetti sauce… But we are still butcher and *charcutier* first and foremost. Or rather: butcher, *charcutier* and cattle breeder. Hendrik, like me, was fascinated by cattle breeding. This is important. It helps you know the beasts properly, you really know what's going on, you respect them. That's really important. About ten years ago, we became interested in the West Flemish Red cattle. This is a breed that closely resembles the Maine-Anjou. It had almost completely disappeared after the war, as most farmers preferred the more profitable Belgian Blue. The West Flemish Red is at home in this region and can benefit from the characteristics of the ecosystem typical of Westhoek countryside. We went looking and found several more of this breed at other farms. In Poperinge. In Diksmuide. Together with some colleagues we took it upon ourselves to save the breed. Hendrik even brought the cow on to the stage at The Flemish Primitives. The result is that now everyone is convinced of the qualities of the animal, and everyone wants this breed."

Hendrik takes over: "The West Flemish Red is a beautiful animal. We were able to make it clear to the breeders that we have to respect the special, distinctive qualities of this breed, which is excellent for both dairy and meat. In the 1960s and 1970s, breeders were genetically engineering the animals to be either dairy or beef cows. The Belgian Blue, for example, is for meat, Holstein for milk… But I don't like that approach. Good meat is good meat! It is important to take your time. A cow must be given time to grow fat. That makes all the difference."

Raymond in the fields behind the farm. "Look how well they look… Yes, as Hendrik says, you have to fatten them gradually, with grass and in the open air. All my cows here have calved at least twice, better yet three times. Being in calf is important to get good meat. After birth, the mother cow produces milk and fat, and so the meat is nicely marbled. Everything contributes to developing better beef. Not a single animal of mine goes to the slaughterhouse before it's six or seven years old. When it comes to quality, nothing is left to chance."

Hendrik: "That comes at a price. The meat is better, but more expensive. But that's the future. In the future, people will eat less meat. I am well aware of that. My father's vision – and mine too, of course – is founded on the logic of sustainable development: eat less, if needs be, but eat better quality!"

Raymond: "You have to teach your customers that. You have to explain it to them. Explain again and again."

Hendrik: "And in the process of explaining, you get hungry. Hungry for that meat or that vegetable. How shall I say it? You just get hungry, you develop a healthy appetite. And you end up understanding why good craft costs a bit more."

9pm. The sun is setting, the wind is rising.

In utter silence, six cows gaze curiously at us. We look back at them. "So," says Raymond, "that's all." In the distance we hear the sound of cars. Then the gate closes again. Raymond asks if I want to see his chicks. "We also should talk about the Mechelen cuckoo," Hendrik sighs. "The Mechelen cuckoo, the real Mechelen cuckoo, has also become a rare thing. I'll explain it to you. Come on in, we'll sit down and I'll tell you…"

Indoors the table is set.

CRAFT

IT'S A MATTER OF SKILL. IT'S ABOUT YOUR HANDS. THE HANDS OF MEN AND WOMEN EXCELLING AT THEIR PROFESSION, MAKING THINGS. IT STARTS WITH THE RAW INGREDIENT THAT BECOMES SOMETHING IN YOUR HANDS. A CRAFTSMAN MAKES SOMETHING AND THEN DISAPPEARS. WHAT HE HAS MADE SPEAKS FOR ITSELF.

WEST FLEMISH RED

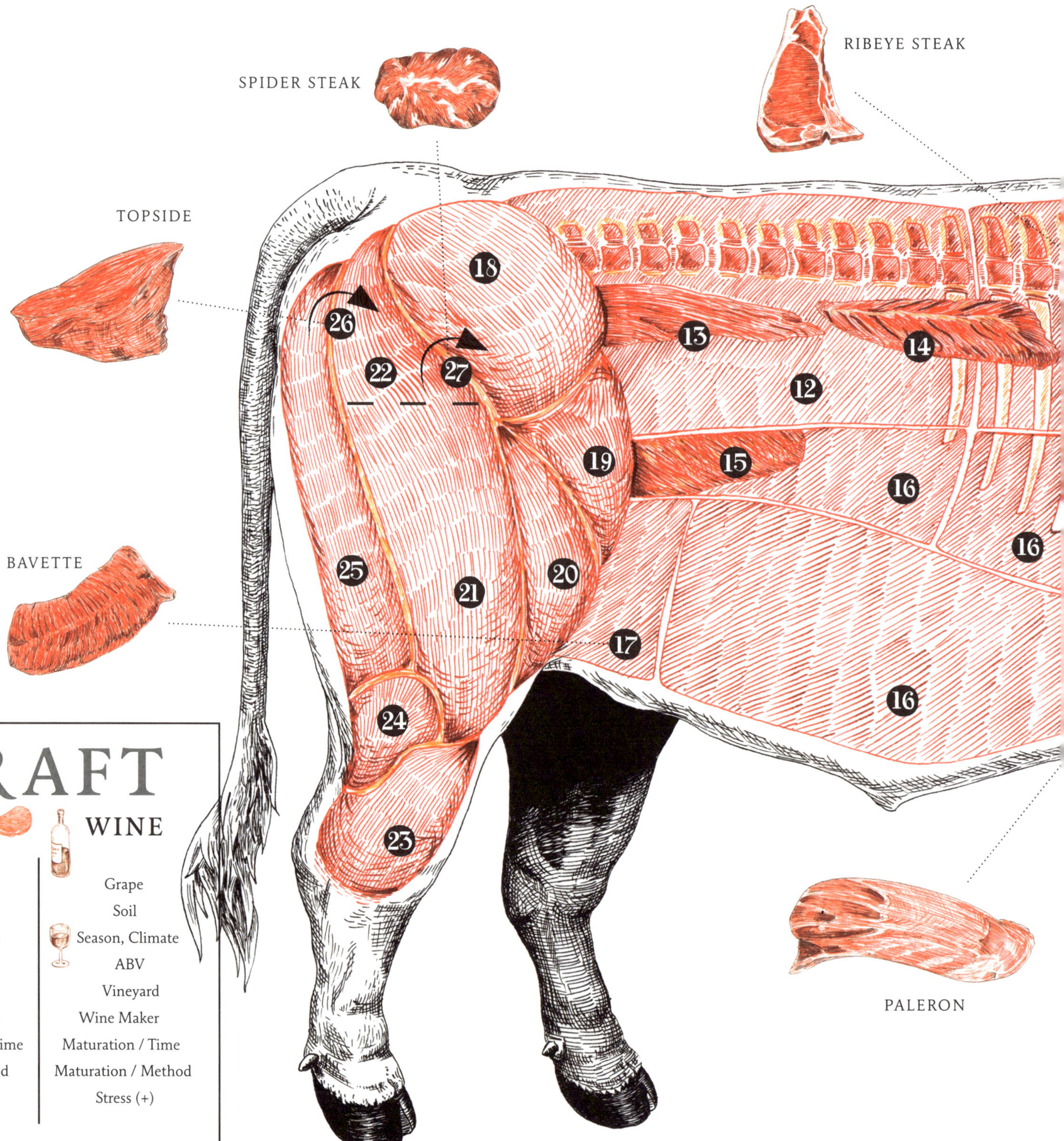

CRAFT

MEAT	WINE
Meat – Breed	Grape
Region, Terroir	Soil
Season, Climate	Season, Climate
Marbling	ABV
Breeder	Vineyard
Meat Processor	Wine Maker
Refining / Drying Time	Maturation / Time
Refining / Method	Maturation / Method
Stress (–)	Stress (+)

DIERENDONCK

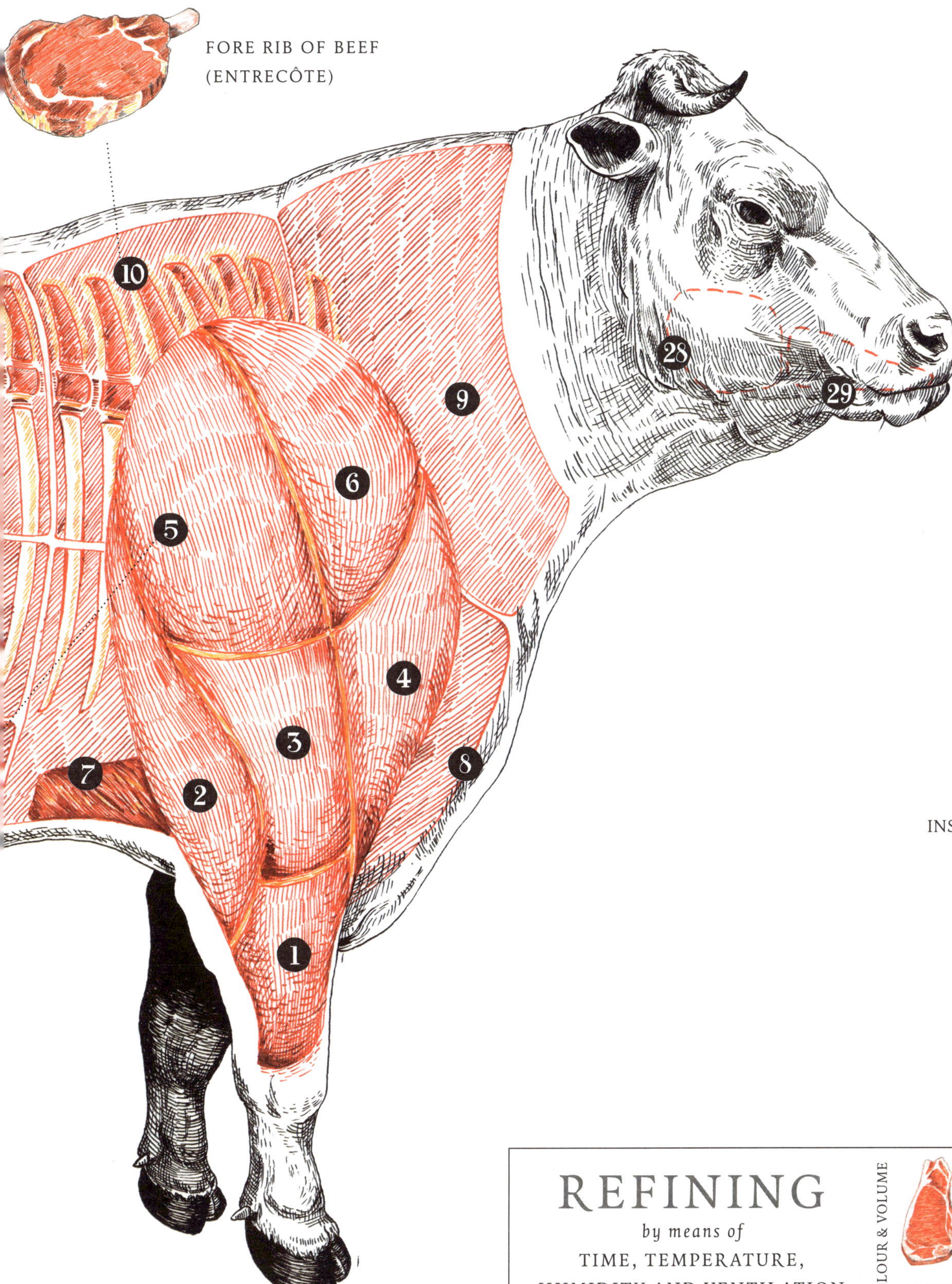

	FRONT SHANK	1
	SHOULDER BALL	2
	CHUCK	3
	CHUCK	4
	PALERON	5
	FALSE FILLET	6
	BRISKET	7
	BREAST	8
	NECK	9
	FORE RIB OF BEEF (ENTRECÔTE)	10
	RIBEYE STEAK	11
	SIRLOIN	12
	TENDERLOIN	13
	HANGER STEAK	14
	SKIRT STEAK	15
FLANK	TOP RIBS	16
	TRIMMED OVAL STEAK	16
	SHORT PLATE	16
	BAVETTE	17
	FULL LOIN AND RUMP	18
	CAP OF RUMP	19
	THICK FLANK KNUCKLE	20
	OUTSIDE FLAT	21
	SILVERSIDE	22
	HIND SHANK	23
	ROYAL ROUND STEAK	24
	FILET D'ANVERS	25
	TOPSIDE	26
	INSIDE THE HIP BONE (SPIDER STEAK)	27
	CHEEK	28
	TONGUE	29

Translator's note
The meat diagram is specific to Dierendonck and the cuts are not always equivalent to British or North American butcher cuts, which also differ by country and region.

REFINING
by means of
TIME, TEMPERATURE,
HUMIDITY AND VENTILATION

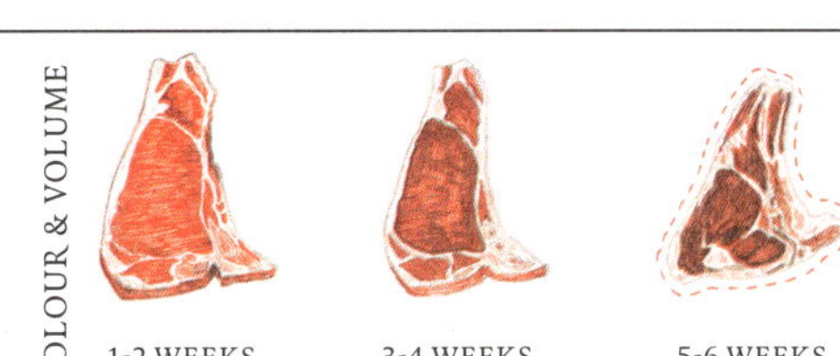

“When I was little, the butcher’s shop did very well, but nothing like its current success.

“My parents worked especially hard during the peak season, from June to early October. In the winter, things quietened down. My father liked to talk to his customers. He explained what he was doing. Why that animal and no other, why that piece and no other. He would give advice. That’s why our customers became regular customers. They knew us and we knew them. My father knew their names and knew a lot of things about them. Because he had time, he was also able to start working in animal husbandry. Now we are livestock farmers, butchers and *charcutiers.*

“From an early age I learned to respect the animals. We’ve always worked with what they now call the ‘nose-to-tail’ method. Because we had to sell our animals, we paid as much attention to the noble parts of the animal as to the less noble, as much to the front quarters as to the rear quarters.

“We also travelled a lot. My father always urged us not to worry about the competition, but to look further afield. Be curious, get to know the livestock farmers. Go to Rungis or to a village a few kilometres from our house. Meet butchers who love their trade. ‘*Tiens,* he makes his black pudding like this. And he does it this way…’ That’s how I got to know butchers who are passionate about their profession. Old-school butchers.

“During the quieter periods in the store, we would explore and get creative. For The Flemish Primitives in 2011, I came up with the idea of curing my West Flemish Red beef sirloin for a month, then salting it and letting it age for another month. I gave it time, that’s how you very slowly develop some powerful meat, with a nutty and buttery taste.

“I wanted to let David Martin from La Paix restaurant taste it. David was the first one in Belgium to start handling meat in a different way. He was the first to age meat here. A friend who had previously worked at Bruneau knew him. We ate together. He tasted it and he liked it. *“Jambon de boeuf rouge de Flandre,”* (red beef ham from Flanders) he said. And so it was! Nobody in Belgium made anything like that. David was the first person to put one of my meat products on his menu. That gave me confidence. Anderlecht, the market, a popular brasserie with a rich history… La Paix is a monument. That was very important to me.”

Ras WEST FLEMISH RED
Lotnr. 150415
Slachtdatum 58 DAYS
Land van afkomst RAYMOND DIERENDONCK

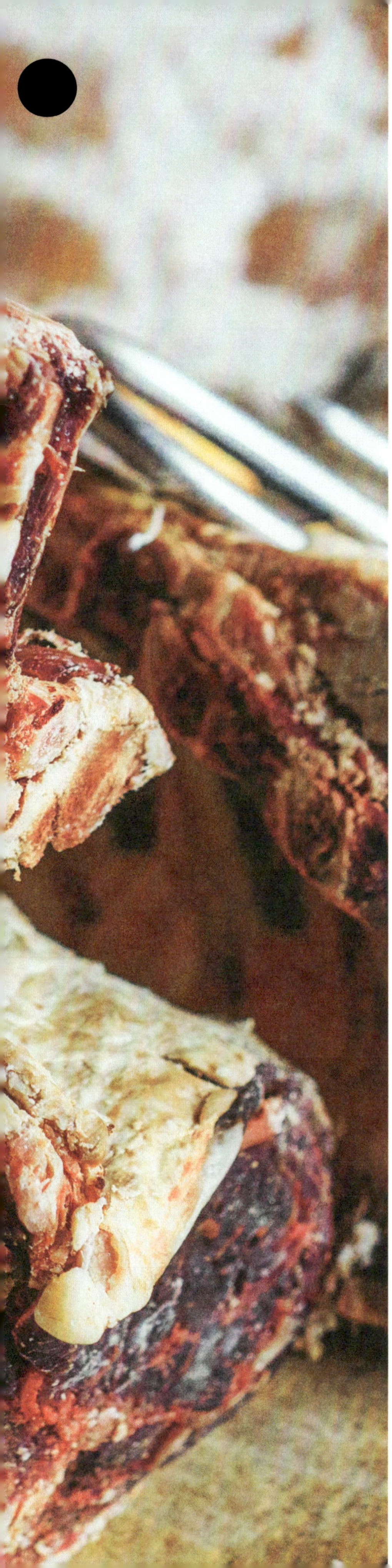

H

“Meat needs to age, but not for too long… Four to six weeks for a beautiful *côte à l’os.* I experimented with that aging process for almost five years before I was satisfied with the results. I knew it would develop more flavour, but that’s not the whole story.

“It starts with the choice of the animal you buy. You must have a pure-bred. A beautiful beast. Not fed with silage, not forcibly fattened up. Then there is too much water in its muscle fibres! The animal needs to have had time outdoors in the fields. And it shouldn’t be too young. It needs to have lived. The meat must have character. Firm meat. The trader should also avoid stress during slaughter. All these things play a role.

“And then your work begins. There is a difference between dry-aging (the technique the British use) and curing. Dry-aging is simply letting the meat dry. The British have beautiful, strong breeds that can produce fat quite young. Animals that spend a lot of time outside. The British were ahead of us when it came to meat treatments. They know how to fatten up their beast. They have been used to eating more meat as far back as the 16th century. On the mainland, this was introduced much later. Cattle were mainly for milk production and were used to work on the land. Strong, muscular animals, but with little fat.

“So letting beef age is something new here. My father didn’t do it. In the old days, in the winter, he would slaughter an animal every three weeks. There were not many customers and the meat had time to rest and soften. It was the natural course of things, two weeks, sometimes three…

“I crossed the channel to see how the British butchers work, but in my shop it needs to be done differently. I let my meat cure through age. I work with meat in the same way that an *affineur* develops his cheese. My meat passes through three different refrigerators. During this process, a fine balance must be maintained between temperature, air circulation and humidity. This is a very, very precise process. The moisture from the meat evaporates and the fat permeates the meat, enriching its flavour. I’ve put lots of hours into my research, and I’ve also focused a lot on the equipment I work with. In 2005 we replaced all our refrigerators. With those old models it was impossible to control the humidity to the fine degree that we do now.

“Great meat is like a great wine or a good cheese, you should enjoy it when it’s at its peak. And a real butcher, a craftsman, knows that moment, knows when the meat is at its best. He takes it out of the fridge at the perfect moment, prepares it and talks about it with his customers: about where it comes from, how it is prepared…”

1
2
3
4
5
6

TRIMMING A RIBEYE STEAK

1 Remove the top from the ribeye.
Cut away the front and back pieces to remove any rot.
2 Make an incision along the full length of the ribs, down to the bone and between the ribs.
3 Free up the ribs with the back of your blade.
4 Knock away the rotten meat with the back of the cleaver.
5 Carve the first côte à l'os.
6 Chop off the heel and back of the vertebra.

RED
Ras
Herford
Lotnr.
Slachtdatum
46 days.
Land van afkomst

H

"With each breed of cattle that you're selling, you have to pay attention to its terroir. You have to look at the producer, of course, but also at the region. The Salers is a dairy cow. And so you fry Salers in butter. The Chianina, a Tuscan breed, is roasted with olive oil and served as tagliata. And not with potatoes: just rocket (arugula), grilled pine nuts and pesto. The Rubia Gallega comes from Galicia. It is best *a la plancha*. The West Flemish Red variety is perfect with butter, it encompasses our roots. Keep in mind the culture of the place the food is coming from. Leaner meats are best cooked in butter while fatty meats do better on the grill. It's different every time.

"A butcher should not only know the different breeds, but also the way they are raised and the soil on which they live. I imagine that on the day when you sell the Aubrac, you also sell the butter that goes with it, and the tallow from the animal to fry it in. And a butcher should be able to talk about the cuts. In France, people are more interested in the different parts of an animal. At the restaurant you can ask for bavette, onglet, *araignée, paleron* or *macreuse*. And the English have their T-bone steak. Why do the English have a preference for that particular piece? And the French for another? And then there is the *aiguillette* (tail piece) and the *culotte* (bottom piece). Which piece does an English roast beef correspond to? And the rump steak? And who knows what a *tendron* or a *macreuse* is? A good butcher needs to know all this.

"We are becoming the sommeliers of meat. The day will come, I think, when a butcher selling a piece of meat will be able to tell you all about its origin and how the animal has been reared, its flavour, and whether the meat has been aged or not. And a vegetable seller will knows where his vegetables come from and how they are grown. You can see it happening already. It's a great way to whet people's appetite – you're making it clear to them that a lot of energy has gone into that product. This gives them a new respect for the breeders and growers."

OEDSLACH

> "OEDSLACH HARKS BACK TO AN ERA WHEN WE TALKED ABOUT PIECES OF MEAT AND CAREFULLY SELECTED THEM FOR MATURING BY CONSIDERING THE COLOUR, MARBLING, AROMA, FAT STRUCTURE, BREED AND AGE OF AN ANIMAL."

Hendrik Dierendonck practically lived in his father Raymond's butcher shop as a child. Really, quite literally. It was a memorable playground too: "I often played hide-and-seek with my brother, hiding between the carcasses in the large refrigerators, with their wooden doors and cork and cement framework. In that cold storage, the very specific smell of the meat left a deep imprint on our young noses. The refrigeration helped the meat develop a unique flavour and had been used by my father for more than 20 years. Little did we know it was called meat aging. In the past, not much meat was sold in winter, so my father often slaughtered only one animal a month. By the end of the month, certain customers would always be asking for a piece of *oedslach,* which is West Flemish for 'old slaughter'. The memory of how that meat was aged in those days, and especially the respect it was treated with, has always stayed with me."

LOT N°
RAS
RIJPING
TERROIR
SELECTION
DIERENDONCK
DIERENDONCK

"THE TEXTURE IS INCREDIBLY TENDER AND THE MEAT TAKES ON A MILDLY CREAMY AND NUTTY FLAVOUR, COMBINED WITH A STRONG AND INTENSE MEATINESS."

"When top chef Sergio Herman told me out of the blue many years later that my meat hadn't tasted the same since moving storage to another location, it opened my eyes. Apparently, without being conscious of it, I had created a specific technique to ripen our meat and I decided to work with it, to fine-tune it. This was gradually achieved through a combination of constantly changing the humidity, temperature and ventilation. A holy trinity, as it were. That process forms a distinct contrast to what is called dry aging, in which the meat rests in dry-aging cabinets.

"The meat I work with to create Oedslach comes from slightly older dual-purpose cows – bred for both their meat and milk. These cattle give a lot of milk, become lean and thus produce beautiful fat. We choose a selection from that meat and let it mature in three different stages and three different refrigerators. First, it hangs in a fridge for ten days, after which the meat is cleaned for the first time. Then it is moved to another refrigerator, where it also hangs, for three to four weeks. A slightly higher temperature accelerates the fermentation; the ripening process. In the final stage, we put the meat in yet another fridge for two to four weeks, where the temperature rises or falls every two hours. After eight to ten weeks you get a nice piece of fermented meat – not overripe, and by no means rotten. When I tasted it for the first time, I was immediately catapulted back to the time when I played hide-and-seek in our old fridges. That's how I came up with the name: Oedslach. As the ultimate tribute to my father.

"Due to changes in the choice of meat, the use of different breeds and the modernisation of refrigerators, we forgot about – and unlearned – this rather particular ripening technique. For years. Yield was given priority over flavour. But more is not better; quite the contrary. I wanted to upend that way of thinking. For me, Oedslach is an innovative project that I will continue to develop in the coming years. At the moment, I'm even studying certain maturation processes with university researchers. In other words, back to the roots is also becoming a bit back to the future.

"Oedslach harks back to an era when we talked about pieces of meat and carefully selected them for maturing by considering the colour, marbling, aroma, fat structure, breed and age of an animal. To fully understand the powerful and intense richness of this meat, you really have to taste it. Oedslach is truly the best meat I've ever eaten. The texture is incredibly tender and the meat takes on a mildly creamy and nutty flavour, combined with a strong and intense meatiness."

RUBIA GALLEGA
(GALICIAN BLONDE)
WEST FLEMISH
RED

HOLSTEIN
SIMMENTAL
DE BAVIÈRE

WEST FLEMISH RED

H

"An almost forgotten beef breed that I revived. It is still our flagship product. Especially because the meat is so pure and because it evokes memories of long-forgotten times. It is a pure, perfect terroir product, which my father Raymond raises himself on our farm. West Flemish Red is a dual-purpose breed, used for both dairy and meat. Thanks to Dierendonck, this breed has experienced something of a resurgence and you now see it here and there in pastures across Flanders. We slaughter the cows when they are five to seven years old and have had two or three calves. The meat has a strong yet refined flavour. It is not excessively marbled but has good fat content. This allows us to age it for three to five weeks."

RUBIA GALLEGA (GALICIAN BLONDE)

"Fifteen years ago, my Belgian-Spanish friend Jean-Paul Perez introduced me to Spanish meat. And what a world of difference – because they have old cows and oxen, in some cases 14 to 18 years old, which pack exceptional flavour. This opened a whole new world to me and also completely changed my ideas about what I do. In the past, we used to slaughter heifers, cows that have calved once, and maidens, cows that have never been with a bull. While I was in Spain, I ate meat that tasted almost like cheese. Meat that had been aged for 150 days. I remember taking a TV team to El Capricho in Jiménez de Jamuz, where a guy called José had oxen, called *buey,* that were 18 and even 21 years old. We discovered the best meat ever in the middle of nowhere!

"Our main mission is to find the right meat and the right suppliers. These days, meat is transported from eastern Europe to Spain, after which it returns to our country only to be sold as 'Spanish meat'. I don't have an issue with eastern European meat, but I want to be sure that I'm getting a proper terroir product. I demand complete transparency when I purchase something to sell in my shop. The Rubia Gallegas we buy are selected especially for us. These are often large cattle, with nice marbling and a dark colour. The meat of this pure breed is not very marbled but it is very dense, meaning it can be aged for ten weeks. I usually recommend Rubia meat to seasoned meat lovers. Sometimes it almost tastes like liver."

NORMANDE

"This breed is comparable to West Flemish Red beef, but it often has a little more intramuscular fat, which explains the creamier flavour. We buy these cows from a small cooperative in Normandy, the region of calvados and cider. These cows are also used for both meat and dairy – the milk is used to make livarot and camembert cheeses. That is why the cows are also a little older, six to seven years. The texture of the meat is coarser, denser and more marbled, and it's aged for at least four weeks. After aging, the meat of a Normande cow has a stronger taste."

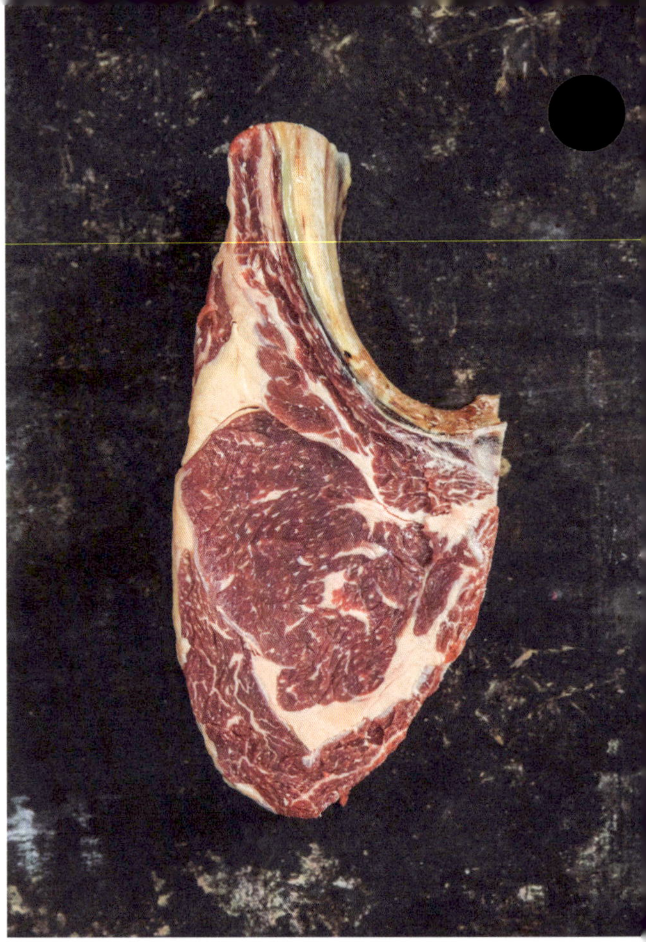

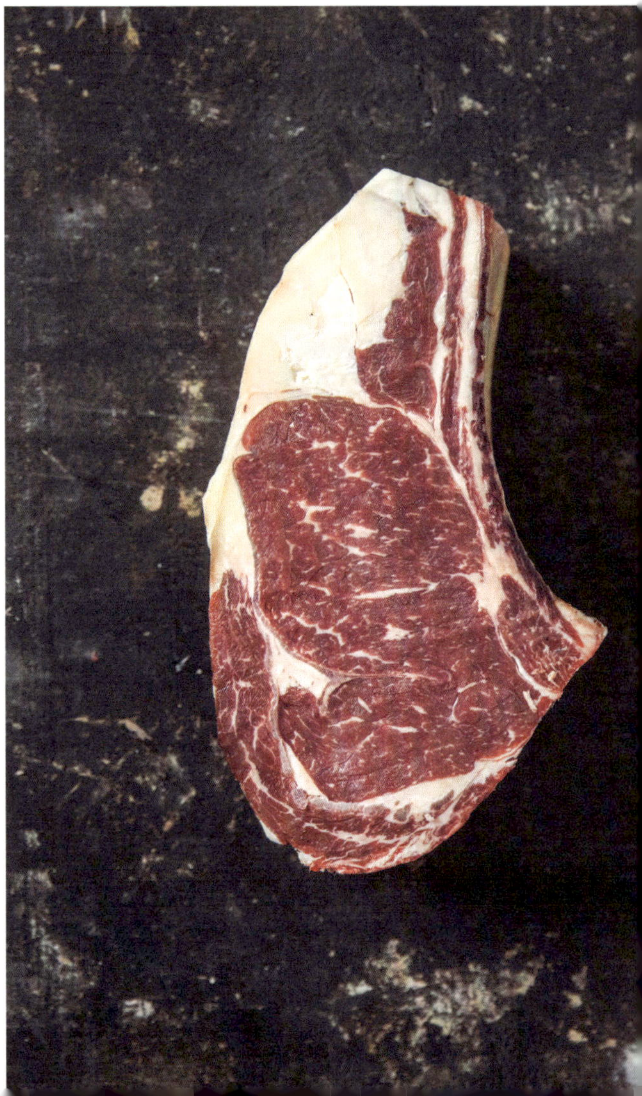

HOLSTEIN

"The northern Dutch Holstein cow is essentially a dairy cow. Originally it was a cross-breed of Friesian and Batavian cows, which produce huge amounts of milk and which many people used to consider inedible. But they're wrong. When the meat is properly aged, it's by far the best meat I've ever tasted. As the cow produces so much milk and is always very skinny, it develops new fat that is very creamy in taste. The more calves the cow has, the creamier and darker the meat. Which explains its incredible marbling. Here, we sometimes call it 'the wagyu of the poor'. The cows are eight to nine years old when we slaughter them, which explains the meat's dense structure with plenty of collagen. We age it for five to eight weeks before consumption."

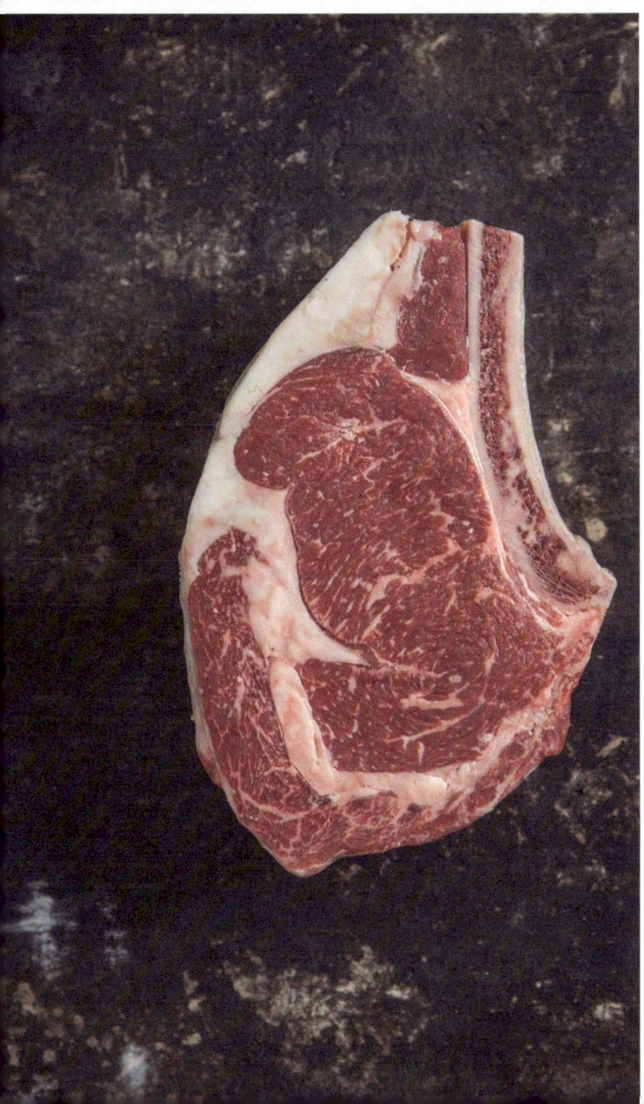

SIMMENTAL DE BAVIÈRE

"The Swiss Simmental breed, sometimes called Swiss Fleckvieh, is also a dual-purpose breed. The roots of this breed lie in Oberland. Nowadays, it is mainly bred in Germany and Austria, in and around Bavaria. This mountain cow is easy to recognise: it's white with light red markings and usually has a large bell around the neck. The French Montbéliarde breed has its origins in Simmental cows, by the way. The meat is often much coarser in texture and has a darkish red colour. It has a pure, strong taste, and experience has taught us that it needs to be aged in a very specific way. Initially, many of my customers said the meat was too tough but we have since solved this problem. As a result, Simmental is now one of the most constant breeds in our range. Times change, eh..."

FRYING & GRILLING

H

“Time only enhances flavour. It’s common sense. And this adage applies equally to the raising, aging and frying of meat. Of course, I’m well aware that sometimes you don’t have all the time in the world. That’s when I like to prepare a delicious entrecôte minute. Thinly sliced and fried in just one minute in good old-fashioned butter for a nice crust.

“Simply delicious, but… I really like to take my time with a thick piece of aged meat, weighing from one kilo up to as much as ten kilos. You have to cook it slowly, at 45-50°C for one to ten hours. Slow-cooking the meat at a low temperature helps to break down the collagen, making the meat even more tender. The fat melts, enhancing the flavour. *Bleu chaud,* just as it should be. Then the meat is grilled over our wood fire, for three to four minutes on each side, until it’s nice and crispy on the outside. At Carcasse, we never ask how you would like us to cook your meat, because we don’t want it to lose any of its flavour or power. Just before serving, we add some melted beef fat and some coarse sea salt. Enjoy your meal!”

RECIPE

Rib of beef, ribeye steak or fillet, 4-5 cm (1.5–2 in) thick.
Cook for 60 minutes at 45-50°C (100–120°F) in a hot air oven.
Massage coarse sea salt into the meat and then grill for 4 to 5 minutes on each side over a hot wood fire or fry in a piping-hot frying pan with butter.
Slice thinly *(émincé)* and serve immediately.

RECIPES

LEVEL OF DIFFICULTY

/ Fast and simple

// For adventurous hobby butchers

/// For experienced butchers

There are a great number of artisanal butcher's shops in Belgium, and each has its own speciality. In Leuven, you have the good luck to have the Rondou butcher's shop, while in Antwerp you'll find the pioneering Benny Vermeulen. But these kinds of places exist across the country – you can find traditional butcher's shops in even the smallest villages. Many of the ingredients for my recipes can be sourced at these wonderful shops, and it really pays to make a detour to visit them. Often, they are not large, shiny shops, but small businesses that, in some cases, have existed for decades. With this book, I pay tribute to their craftsmanship, originality and passion.

RIB OF BEEF IN HAY

H

“Rib of beef in hay is a real treat and you can impress your friends with it. In days gone by, I'd seen farmers cover the pig with hay after it was slaughtered and set it on fire. I had wondered what it was good for. I decided to experiment myself, by mixing hay and fat together. And that's how the recipe Aged Rib of Beef in Hay was born (see p. 129).

“It's a bit fiddly, I'll admit, but it's great. The hay has a light smoky fragrance that goes well with the taste of aged meat.”

AGED RIB OF BEEF IN HAY

24 H

1 large *côte à l'os*,
ribeye or tenderloin
(of your preferred breed)
melted beef fat with hay (see p. 131)
coarse sea salt
extra dried hay

Preferably use a piece of meat that has already matured and not been cleaned.

Equipment
hook
rope
aluminium foil

Quantity
depends on the piece of meat

Melt the beef fat with hay and add salt. Brush the meat with the fat and hay. Repeat this step 3 times.

Take some more hay, mix it with the remaining fat and pat it firmly on to the piece of meat, so that it is completely covered.

If possible, leave this in a ventilated fridge overnight (or 2 or 3 nights), then remove the piece of meat from the fridge about 5 hours before cooking.

Set the hay on fire (if possible in the open air): the fire will basically burn away all the overripe pieces on the outside, and the fat will work its way into the meat.

Now you can clean up the front and back of the meat a little and fry the meat in one piece, or cut it into a bunch of steaks and grill them.

The flavour of the powerful meat and hay delivers a wonderful tasting experience.

H

“I met Sergio Herman at The Flemish Primitives in 2011. We had brought one of our own West Flemish Red cattle right on to the stage. It took some artful preparation, but I was able to really illustrate our view of the butcher’s trade. I gave demonstrations with the West Flemish Red breed, a Rubia Gallega sirloin steak, a Wagyu and a rib of beef from Giorgio Nava’s farm in South Africa.

“Sergio invited me to his place and I drove over with a van full of different cuts of meat. We tasted everything, but he wanted something different. That’s when I thought of the *paleron,* the yoke. It is little known and is mainly used for pot roast. It’s part of the forequarter. Nowadays, people prefer the nobler, more tender pieces of the hindquarter. The front part of a cow has more work to do. But when we’re talking about a beautiful, well-bred cow, you can also use a piece of the forequarter for a roast. It’s not very tender, but it’s interesting. A muscle that works, is full of blood. He liked the idea.

“We made a few attempts, but the meat never got tender enough. Then I got the idea to let it cure on the leg. Something like that is not done, you don’t let a piece of the shoulder age. But after several attempts, we arrived at a texture and taste that he approved of. He then created an incredible dish that he called ‘cow in meadow’. He put the *paleron* on a barbecue on the table in a Michelin three-star restaurant. The customer was given a plate with a crown of vegetables representing barbed wire. You had to take the meat from the middle of the table and then bring it to pasture. Classic Sergio!”

AGED BEEF FAT MELTED WITH BUTTER AND HAY

Time: 30 minutes – Quantity: 300 g (10.5 oz)

Ingredients: 200 g (7 oz) melted beef fat, hay, 100 g (3.5 oz) butter, coarse salt and pepper

Dry out the hay for 10 minutes in a preheated oven at 180°C (350°F). Melt the butter and the beef fat together. Add the hay to this fat, sauté briefly, put the lid on and season with coarse salt and pepper of your choice. Remove the hay. Place the fat in a preserving jar and cover with hay. Store in a cool place.

AGED BONE-IN RIBSTEAK OR RIBEYE

HOW DO I COOK MY MEAT?

1 H

4 P

1 big bone-in ribsteak or ribeye
(4–5 cm [1.5–2 in] thick,
± 1.5 kg [3 lb 5 oz] with bone)
coarse sea salt
freshly ground pepper
olive oil

The meat should have been aged for 3 to 4 weeks.

Warm up the meat for an hour in a convection oven at 50°C (120°F).

Leave your oven ajar so that the air circulates.

This will give the meat a crisp burnished crust when it's fried.

Season the meat with coarse sea salt, pepper and olive oil. Rub it in lightly. Fry or grill over a high heat for 3–4 minutes on each side, depending on its thickness. Chop off the bone and fry for another 30 seconds on each side.

Carve the ribeye into thin slices and scatter coarse sea salt on top.

GENTLY AGED AND SMOKED 'PALERON'

ON THE BONE

0.5 H *

4 P

Preparation aging and smoking for experienced cooks: let the meat cure for 3 to 4 weeks at 70% humidity in a dry, ventilated fridge. Smoke the chuck meat for 2 hours at 28°C (80°F), bone it and clean it.

Smoking for the hobby butcher: buy the meat aged and peeled, then cold-smoke it for an hour on your barbecue with some beech wood. Smoking and curing gives the meat a richer taste sensation.

Method: bake the shoulder blade bone in the oven at a high temperature – 20 minutes at 250°C (480°F) will ensure that the bone is nicely browned for use when serving. Let it cool.

Preheat the oven to 50°C (120°F) for about 30 minutes and warm the peeled and smoked meat for 30 minutes.
Pay attention: don't let the heat exceed 58°C (135°F), or the meat will start cooking too soon, and we want to avoid that.

Now gently rub the warm beef shoulder with the sea salt and coarsely ground pepper. Melt the hay fat slowly in the pan until it starts to turn light brown, then place the meat in the hot pan. Now apply the 20-second rule: turn the meat every 20 seconds, which will give you a nice crisp crust. Do this for 3 to 4 minutes and then remove the meat from the pan.

Slice the meat neatly and arrange on the baked shoulder blade. Finish with a few spoons of the beef fat and a pinch of coarse sea salt.

Serve this dish on the bone for a beautiful presentation of this richly flavoured meat.

1 cured small shoulder cut, *paleron,* peeled, weighing 800 g (1 lb 12 oz) to 1 kg (2 lb 4 oz) (ask your butcher for the shoulder blade bone too)
coarse sea salt
crushed black pepper
melted beef fat with hay (see p. 131)

Equipment
smoker
oven
pan
barbecue with beech wood lid

*** Level**
level 2 if you buy it already aged
level 1 if you buy it already aged, smoked and boned by the butcher

*** Time**
30 minutes if aged and smoked by your butcher
1.5 hours if you want to try smoking it on your barbecue yourself

WEST FLEMISH RED SHORT RIBS

SLOWLY BRAISED

24 H

4-6 P

Arrange the ribs in a large casserole dish.

Cover them with the onions, crushed garlic, carrots, salt and pepper, olive oil, the good beer (and some for the cook) and some of the beef fond. Divide the butter evenly across the ribs.

All this can now braise in the oven very slowly: 5 to 6 hours at 110°C (230°F).

Every 20 to 30 minutes, baste the meat with the gravy, which is now a nicely balanced mix of the fond, butter, beer and so on. The ribs will become crispy-brown, but the constant basting will keep them juicy and lightly caramelised at the same time. The fat from the beef ribs will also acquire great flavour.

Let the ribs rest overnight in the fridge.

Cut the meat into nice even pieces that can be presented on the rib.

Bake these in the oven for another hour at 110°C (230°F) and brush them with the beef gravy from your roasting pan. Now carefully present them on the bone and serve.

So tasty you'll be licking your fingers!

4 fatty beef ribs
2 onions
4 cloves of garlic
4 carrots
thyme
bay leaf
olive oil
400 ml (13.5 fl oz) beef fond
(see p. 243)
pepper
coarse salt
thyme
rosemary
750 ml (25 fl oz) dark regional beer
300 g (10.5 oz) butter

Equipment

casserole dish or roasting pan

SPIDER STEAK, SKIRT STEAK AND BAVETTE

FORGOTTEN CUTS OF BEEF

2 H

butter or fat
pepper
salt
meat cut of your choice

For the red wine sauce
1 shallot
1 glass of red wine
1 knob of butter
pepper
salt
100 ml (3.5 fl oz) beef fond
(see p. 243)

Quantity
depends on the cut

Remove the meat from the refrigerator for an hour to let it reach room temperature.
Warm it for an hour in a preheated oven at 50°C (120°F).
Season with salt and pepper.
Melt the fat in a hot pan.
Sear the meat over a high heat for 3 minutes on each side.

It's delicious with red wine sauce: sauté the finely chopped shallot.
Remove the meat from the pan.
Deglaze the pan with fond and red wine.
Reduce the sauce.
Add the shallot and season with salt and pepper.

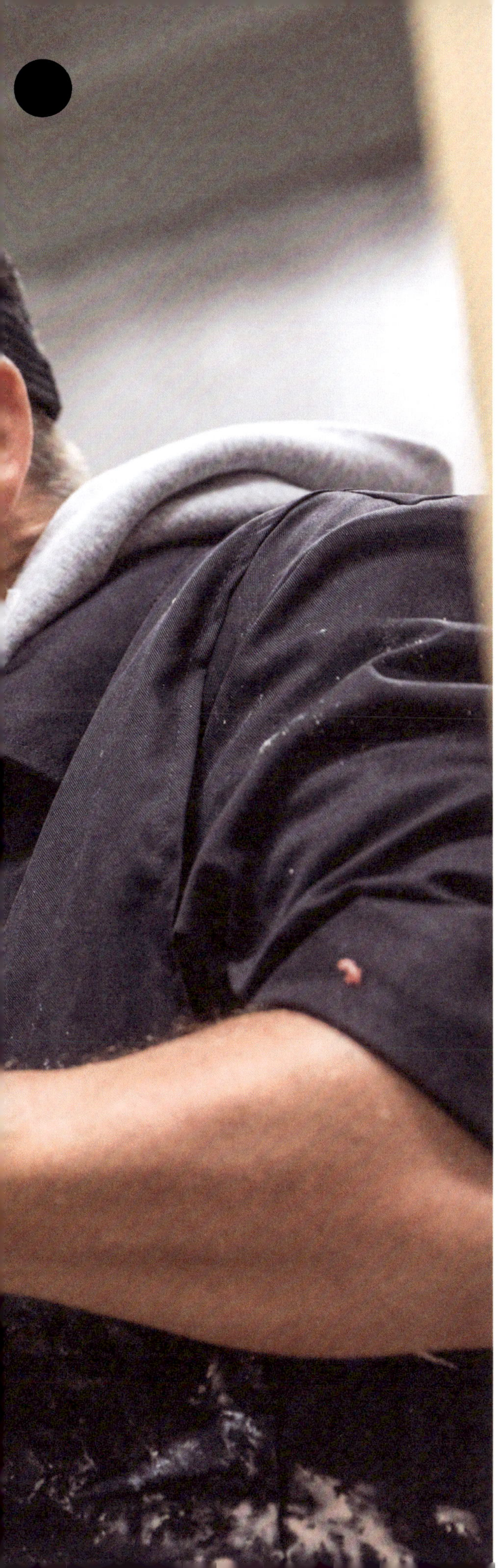

DRY-AGED RIBEYE

H

“I first prepared a dry-aged ribeye of beef (or entrecôte) during The Flemish Primitives event in 2011. I was already experimenting a lot at the time. Since then several chefs – including Peter Goossens and Sergio Herman – have put dry-aged ribeye on their menu. The beef rib – a carefully selected sirloin steak of West Flemish Red beef – is aged for one month. This is done according to a specific cycle, a special traditional process that I developed myself and which is comparable to the process for ripening cheese.
It is based on a continuous interaction of temperature and moisture. After a month, the meat almost starts to ferment. The enzymes give the meat a specific taste. Then the meat is deboned, or ‘trimmed’. We then dry-salt it with herbs and sea salt (half coarse and half fine sea salt) and vacuum-seal it. And then we wait another month. It’s a very slow process.
After four, sometimes even five weeks, we unpack the meat and let it sit for another four to six weeks. This is called dry-aging. The entire process can last between three and four months, in other words.
But the flavours are amazing.

“A dry-aged ribeye steak tastes very meaty because of the aging and the maturation, adding a nutty, buttery flavour to the meat. At Carcasse, we combine this complex flavour with some smoky mayonnaise and pickled vegetables. Dry-aged ribeye has become one of Dierendonck’s trade- marks. Many Belgian and international chefs are interested in our meat.
In addition to dry-aged rib of Belgian Red beef we now also use Holstein beef.”

DRY-AGED WEST FLEMISH RED ENTRECÔTE

WITH HERBS, TOAST AND SMOKED MAYONNAISE

0.5 H

4 P

Slice the entrecôte very thinly and bring up to room temperature.

Steep the sprigs of dill in iced water for a few minutes then allow to dry on a damp kitchen towel. Cut the chives into batonettes.

Combine all the ingredients for the awesome vinaigrette and mix well (always mix again just before using).

Put all the ingredients for the pickling liquid in a large pot and bring to the boil for a few seconds. Let it sit for 1 hour and then strain.

Slice the shallot into rings and immerse in the pickling liquid. Cover and leave overnight.

Thinly slice the bread, drizzle with olive oil and a pinch of salt and bake in the oven for 2 minutes at 200°C (390°F) between two sheets of baking parchment.

Place all the ingredients for the mayonnaise (except for the grapeseed oil) into a blender or Thermomix bowl and mix for a few seconds. Gradually add the grapeseed oil until the mayonnaise has the desired texture. Transfer to a piping bag.

Arrange the meat on a plate and drizzle with olive oil and a pinch of pepper. Add the dill and chives to the vinaigrette and also drizzle over the meat. Arrange a few shallot rings on top and garnish with grated parmesan and the toast.

80 g (2.8 oz) dry-aged West Flemish Red entrecôte
2 sprigs of fresh dill
4 chives
1 shallot
small loaf of white bread
a pinch of pepper
good olive oil
small piece of parmesan cheese

Awesome vinaigrette
100 ml (3.5 fl oz) good olive oil
100 ml (3.5 fl oz) sushi vinegar
110 ml (3.8 fl oz) Forum chardonnay vinegar
a pinch of pepper
a pinch of salt

Pickling liquid for the shallots
(basic pickling liquid)
200 ml (7 fl oz) sugar water
230 ml (8 fl oz) Forum chardonnay vinegar
200 ml (7 fl oz) sushi vinegar
a few sprigs of fresh thyme
10 peppercorns
a pinch of salt
3 star anise
3 juniper berries
1 tbsp coriander seeds
1 tbsp fennel seeds

Smoked mayonnaise
basic mayonnaise (see p. 243)
2 tbsp Sosa smoke powder

Many butchers use classic steak or fatty rump meat for their tartare. Some even opt for filet mignon. But filet is too tender. Too expensive. They even ask me for onglet. That's idiotic. There is too little onglet for that. On a 550-kg cow, there is 600 g of onglet. You understand? 600 g! I think bavette is better suited. There is 3–4 kg per animal. It's cheaper, but more importantly, it's better. A butcher has to explain such things. He needs to know all those pieces, the work they did in life and how to cut them up. Why is a hindquarter softer? Why does a cow have to graze? A butcher has to ask questions. I also learned that from my father. He would ask, 'What do you want this meat for? What do you like?' And then he would explain. For hours he explained.

"And why do I prefer bavette? Because it is a piece that is perfect for a tartare, with a rich taste and nice texture. You have a bite, you have something to chew on. It is juicy and fibrous flesh. It contains less blood than onglet, but still, straight from the first bite it is an explosion of flavour. A bavette that has been cured only briefly, for seven to ten days. You cut it by hand. With a sharp knife. That's my father's second lesson: how to sharpen knives. In a butcher's shop, just like in a kitchen, you need knives that cut. If a blade doesn't cut, you're pressing too hard, crushing the fibres and losing juices. You cut the meat first with the grain, then against the grain. Olive oil, salt and pepper. Not too much. You can use a little grilled marrow to add fat and flavour. We did that at Omnivore with Nick Bril from The Jane in Antwerp. A small detail that makes a big difference. Enhance the creaminess and taste of your meat: tartare is for real meat eaters."

CUTTING TARTARE FROM BAVETTE

1. First cut the meat into slices following the grain.
2. Slice the meat again, now against the grain.
3. Place the slices on top of each other and cut into strips, following the grain again.
4. To finish, cut the meat into little cubes.

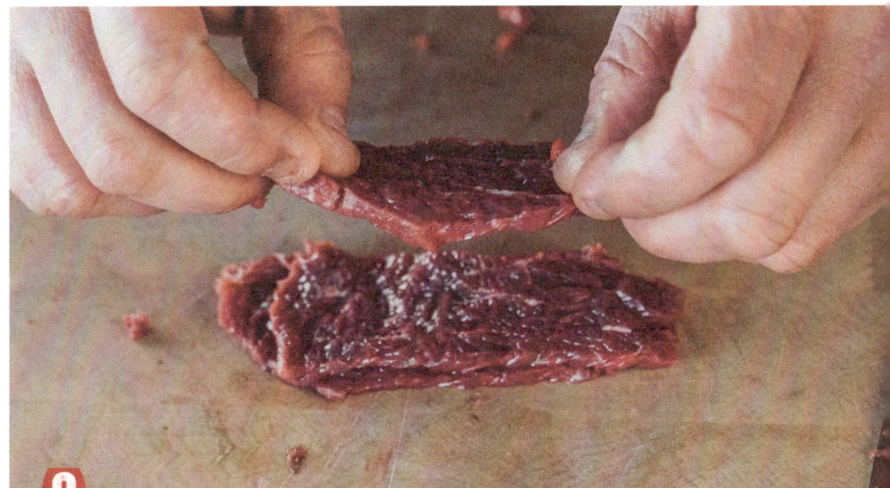

BEEF TARTARE

WITH MARROW

1 H

4 P

600 g (1 lb 5 oz) beef bavette
2 egg yolks
1 shallot
1 tbsp (15 ml) mustard
Tabasco
2 tbsp (30 ml) Worcestershire sauce
salt
parsley
pepper
2 tbsp (30 ml) capers
olive oil
4 beef marrowbones
(cut in half lengthwise)
beef stock

Boil the marrowbones in the stock for 20 minutes. Remove the bones from the stock, scoop out the marrow and let it cool. Grill the bones for 4 minutes on the barbecue or in the oven. Peel the shallot. Finely chop the shallot, capers and parsley.

Cut the meat tartare with your knife (see p. 147).
Mix the meat with the marrow, egg yolks, finely chopped shallot, mustard and parsley.

Season with Worcestershire sauce, pepper, salt, olive oil and Tabasco. Spoon the tartare into the marrowbones and top with the capers. Serve.

ROASTED MARROWBONES

NICE AND FATTY FOR MY TARTARE

1 H

4 beef marrowbones
(cut in half lengthwise)
beef stock
coarse salt

Equipment
barbecue

Boil the marrowbones in the stock for 20 minutes.
Remove from the broth and let cool.
Cook on the barbecue for no more than 1 minute on the marrow side.
Flip and cook for a further 3 minutes.
Finish with a pinch of coarse salt and serve immediately.

GRILLED MARROWBONE

WITH GREMOLATA

0.5 H

2 P

Cook the marrowbone for ± 15 minutes in the oven at 190°C (375°F).

For the gremolata, finely chop the flat-leaf parsley and combine with the olive oil, garlic, zest and juice of the lemon, and add a pinch of salt.

Toast the bread slices in the oven at 220°C (430°F) until nice and crispy.

Arrange the gremolata on the marrowbone, serve with the toast and garnish with grated parmesan.

1 marrowbone, halved lengthwise
6 wafer-thin slices of white bread
piece of parmesan cheese

Gremolata
½ bunch of flat-leaf parsley
3 tbsp good olive oil
1 clove of garlic, minced
zest and juice of 1 lemon
a pinch of salt

DEEP-FRIED CALF'S BRAINS

WITH CHORON MAYONNAISE

1.5 H

4 P

2 calf's brains
flour
3 eggs
panko
a pinch of pepper
a pinch of salt
lemon zest
fleur de sel

Choron mayonnaise
30 g (1 oz) ketchup
25 g (2 tbsp) concentrated tomato purée
20 g (0.7 oz) egg white
20 ml (0.7 fl oz) sushi vinegar
juice of 1 lime
30 ml (1 fl oz) tarragon vinegar
a pinch of xanthan gum
15 g (1 tbsp) mustard
a pinch of salt
800 ml (28 fl oz) grapeseed oil
some ice-cold water

Soak the calf's brains overnight in cold water to drain the blood.

Rinse, then simmer for 10 minutes in salted water (don't boil). Drain and plunge into iced water. Beat the 3 eggs and season with salt and pepper.

Divide the brains into portions and coat first with sieved flour, then with egg, and then with panko. Refrigerate for 2 hours so they're nice and cold and easier to fry.

Deep-fry at 180°C (350°F) until golden brown.

Combine all the ingredients (except the grapeseed oil) for the choron mayonnaise, then whisk in the oil.

Garnish the brains with the lemon zest and fleur de sel. Serve the mayonnaise on the side.

TÊTE DE VEAU (CALF'S HEAD) EN TORTUE

4 H

8 P

Place the calf's head and all the ingredients for the stock in a large casserole, cover with water and simmer for 3-3.5 hours until you can prick it easily with a pointed knife. Remove the calf's head from the stock, cool slightly, remove from the strings and peel the tongue. Then chop everything finely (you can also chop it coarsely), transfer to a terrine and weigh down. Let it set in the fridge and then cut portions to the desired size. Season with salt and pepper and fry until crisp in olive oil.

Cut the pearl onions and gherkins in half.

Combine the mayonnaise and tarragon leaves to make the tarragon cream, then whisk in the grapeseed oil.

For the tomato sauce: gently cook the onions, garlic, thyme and oregano with some salt and pepper. Add the san marzano tomatoes. Add the sugar, let it melt and pour over some red wine. Reduce, then stir in the Madeira wine, and reduce again. Then add the tinned tomatoes and the stock and let simmer for ± 1 hour. Mix well and strain through a fine sieve. Season with salt and pepper and stir in a dash of Madeira wine, if necessary.

Fry the quail egg in some butter. Garnish with a few sprigs of tarragon.

H

“A largely forgotten cut of meat, which we want to put back on the map at Carcasse. In a sense, it's what we do best: create a new, contemporary take on old-fashioned recipes and old-fashioned charcuterie. Together, the master chef and butcher play vital roles in this. And this combination makes it fun and interesting for everyone. The old-fashioned calf's head is cooked very slowly, in a tomato sauce. We combine this with breaded peas and serve it with a luke-warm poached egg on top. Reviving a classic dish with a few new flavours – this is typical of what we do at Carcasse. We want to introduce the younger generation to new discoveries, which they would otherwise never get the chance to taste.”

deboned calf's head with tongue
3 pearl onions
baby gherkins
1 quail egg
a few sprigs of tarragon

Stock

2 onions
1 leek
3 carrots
1 bulb of garlic
10 black peppercorns
3 celery stalks
3 star anise
a large pinch of salt
a few sprigs of thyme

Tarragon cream

basic mayonnaise (see p. 243)
80 g (3 oz) tarragon leaves

Tomato sauce

3 cevenne onions, finely chopped
2 cloves of garlic, finely chopped
6 sprigs of thyme, leaves only
4 sprigs of oregano
a large pinch of salt and pepper
4 san marzano tomatoes, diced
50 g (1.8 oz) sugar
400 g (14 oz) tinned tomatoes
150 ml (5 fl oz) calf's head stock
some red wine
some Madeira wine

VITELLO TONNATO CARCASSE

0.5 H

2 P

4 good slices of vitello/veal
1 slice of white bread
3 cherry tomatoes
purple shiso leaves
lime cress
lime zest

Tuna sauce
150 g (5.3 oz) drained tuna steak (tinned)
150 g (5.3 oz) chicken stock (see p. 243)
5 anchovies soaked in milk
1 tsp capers
20 g (0.7 oz) egg yolk
10 ml (1 tbsp) tarragon vinegar
10 ml (1 tbsp) sushi vinegar
a pinch of salt
juice of 1 lime
220 ml (8 fl oz) grapeseed oil

Avocado cream
2 avocados
1 tsp greek yoghurt
juice of ½ lime
a pinch of salt

Fry the bread until crisp in butter and transfer to kitchen paper.

Put all the ingredients for the tuna sauce (except for the grapeseed oil) in a blender. Mix well and then add the grapeseed oil.

Put all the ingredients for the avocado cream in a blender and mix until smooth. Transfer to a piping bag.

Quarter the cherry tomatoes.

Spread the tuna sauce on the toast, place the veal on top and garnish with the avocado cream, cherry tomatoes, shiso, lime cress, lime zest and a pinch of pepper.

MY HOME-MADE 'FRIKANDEL'

FOR ROSIE AND FONS

1 H

1 KG 2.2 LB

800 g (1 lb 12 oz) minced pork (80% meat / 20% fat)
200 g (7 oz) finely ground beef
100 ml (3.5 fl oz) vegetable stock (see p. 243)
2 handfuls of breadcrumbs
18 g (1½ tbsp) sea salt
3 g (½ tsp) pepper from the mill
a pinch of nutmeg
a pinch of mace
1 tbsp (15 ml) mustard
a handful of coarsely chopped parsley
1 farm egg
1.5 litres (2 pt 13) vegetable stock

Mix all the ingredients in a large mixing bowl into a beautifully smooth dough.

Wet your hands, take a handful of minced meat and roll it, on a work surface, into a *frikandel* with a diameter of 3 cm (just over 1 in).

Poach the *frikandel* in the stock at 74°C (165°F) for 15 minutes. Let them cool completely on paper towels and place in the fridge overnight. Fry or grill on the barbecue.

Tip: *moisten your hands in cold water, it will help you roll a nice even sausage.*

COARSE-GROUND BURGERS

OF WEST FLEMISH RED BEEF

1 H

4 P

Melt the butter and fat until lukewarm. Let it cool for a while, if necessary. Mix the meat with the Worcestershire sauce, melted fat and spices. Add the egg at the end to bind all the ingredients together. Season with sea salt and freshly ground pepper. Divide the whole into portions of about 160 g (5.5 oz) each. Shape into burgers about 2 cm (1 in) thick.

Note: don't press down too hard on the burgers, so that they keep a nice structure after frying. Cook the burgers for 2 minutes on each side, on the barbecue, under the grill or in a frying pan with a knob of farm butter. Let them rest briefly, then serve.

***Tip:** the melted butter, beef fat and coarse structure of the minced meat ensure that the meat remains juicy after cooking and the pure meat flavour comes out better. Personally, I like to eat my burgers with a rustic crispy-toasted bun and home-made barbecue sauce. Optional extras are lettuce, tomato and red onion.*

THE DIERENDONCK BARBECUE SAUCE THAT PACKS A PUNCH

Time: 30 minutes – Quantity: about 500 ml (17 fl oz)

Heat the olive oil in a pan over a gentle heat. Peel and finely chop the onion and crush the garlic. Sauté the garlic and onion in the olive oil and add the spices. Tip: make sure that the onion is sufficiently sautéed, otherwise the sauce will taste of raw onion. Pour in the cider vinegar and apple juice, then reduce by a third. Add the elderberry syrup, ketchup and mustard and let it cook for 5 minutes over a low heat. Blend the sauce in a blender until smooth and pass through a sieve. Pour into a 1-litre bottle. You can store the sauce in an airtight bottle or jar in the fridge for 1–2 weeks.

1 kg (2 lb 4 oz) coarsely (5 mm) minced beef
(85% meat / 15% fat, preferably pieces from the neck because of their firmer structure and full flavour)
50 g (1.8 oz) farm butter
50 g (1.8 oz) melted beef fat
Worcestershire sauce
1 fresh egg
16 g (0.5 oz) sea salt
freshly ground pepper
1 flat tsp ground paprika
a pinch of cayenne pepper

Barbecuesaus Dierendonck

25 ml (0.8 fl oz) 'Dierendonck' olive oil
1 onion
1 garlic clove
3 g (½ tsp) fennel seed
3 g (½ tsp) coriander seed
3 g (½ tsp) celery seed
3 g (½ tsp) mustard seed
3 g (½ tsp) freshly ground black pepper
75 ml (2.5 fl oz) apple juice
75 ml (2.5 fl oz) cider vinegar
50 g (1.8 oz) mustard
60 ml (2 fl oz) elderberry syrup
250 ml (9 fl oz) ketchup
18 g (1½ tbsp) (smoked) sea salt

HOT DOGS

BOYS WILL BE BOYS

24 H

5 KG
11 LB

Start by making the basic dough.

Put in the professional bowl cutter: ⅓ of the ice with ⅓ of the minced meat and all the spices, keeping it under 2°C (36°F). Add the collar bacon, ⅓ of the ice, ⅓ of the minced meat and the frozen milk. Set the cutter as fine as possible and keep at 10°C (50°F).

Now add the rest of the ice and minced meat, and continue chopping, not exceeding 14°C (55°F). Add the 500 g of minced pork, the mustard and coarsely chopped parsley and mix into a homogeneous dough. Fill the sausage casings and portion to your preferred length. Leave to rest overnight.

Smoke for 1.5 hours at 45°C (110°F), then poach in the vegetable stock for 15 minutes at 74°C (165°F). Immediately cool in iced water.

1 kg (2 lb 4 oz) minced beef and pork
500 g (1 lb 2 oz) minced pork
500 ml (17 fl oz) frozen milk
500 ml (17 fl oz) ice shavings
1 kg (2 lb 4 oz) ground collar bacon
1 garlic clove
18 g (1½ tbsp) sodium nitrite per kg (2 lb 4 oz)
5 g (1 tsp) pepper per kg (2 lb 4 oz)
5 g (1 tsp) nutmeg
5 g (1 tsp) cardamom
2.5 g (½ tsp) allspice
1 tbsp (15 ml) mustard
fresh parsley
vegetable stock (see p. 243)
sheep casings (diameter 26–28 mm / 1 in)
3 onions
a knob of butter
8 buns
mustard
Barbecue sauce

Equipment
sausage stuffer machine
powerful cutter (can also be done with a meat grinder)
smoke cabinet

Tip: *don't let the stock boil, as the sausages will burst. To finish, grill on the barbecue or fry in a pan with a knob of butter.*

Tip for serving the hot dogs: *fry finely chopped onions in a knob of butter and let them caramelise. Place the hot dog in a tasty bun and top with caramelised onions, mustard and home-made barbecue sauce (see p. 160).*

Tip: *it's best if the hot dogs are dry on the outside before smoking; this way they absorb the flavour well and will have an attractive colour. If you don't have a smoke cabinet at home, you can easily make one with an old barrel or locker – you can find the wildest tips for this on the internet!*

BRAISED VEAL SHANK

OLD SCHOOL WITH MUSTARD AND DARK BEER

6 H

4 P

veal shank for 4 people (ask your butcher to carve the leg separating it at the top for presentation)
mustard
3 carrots
2 shallots
butter
olive oil
400 ml (14 fl oz) veal stock (see p. 243)
200 g (7 oz) farm butter
330 ml (12 fl oz) of regional dark craft beer
thyme
pepper
salt

Equipment
roasting pan

Rub the veal shanks with mustard.

Place them standing up in a roasting pan and season with coarse sea salt and pepper. Roughly chop the carrots and shallots and arrange around the meat in the pan. Add a dash of olive oil, 100 g (3.5 oz) of butter in cubes, the veal stock and the beer. Season with pepper, sea salt and thyme.

Preheat the oven to 110°C (230°F), if possible setting it to 20% humidity (alternatively, you can place a pot of water in the oven). Bake the veal shanks in the oven for 5–6 hours. Every half hour, ladle the pan's juices over the shanks, which will give you a nice, crispy crust.

Remove the shanks from the oven when the meat is nice and tender and serve just like that, in its own gravy.

Delicious with home-made ratatouille!

PIG

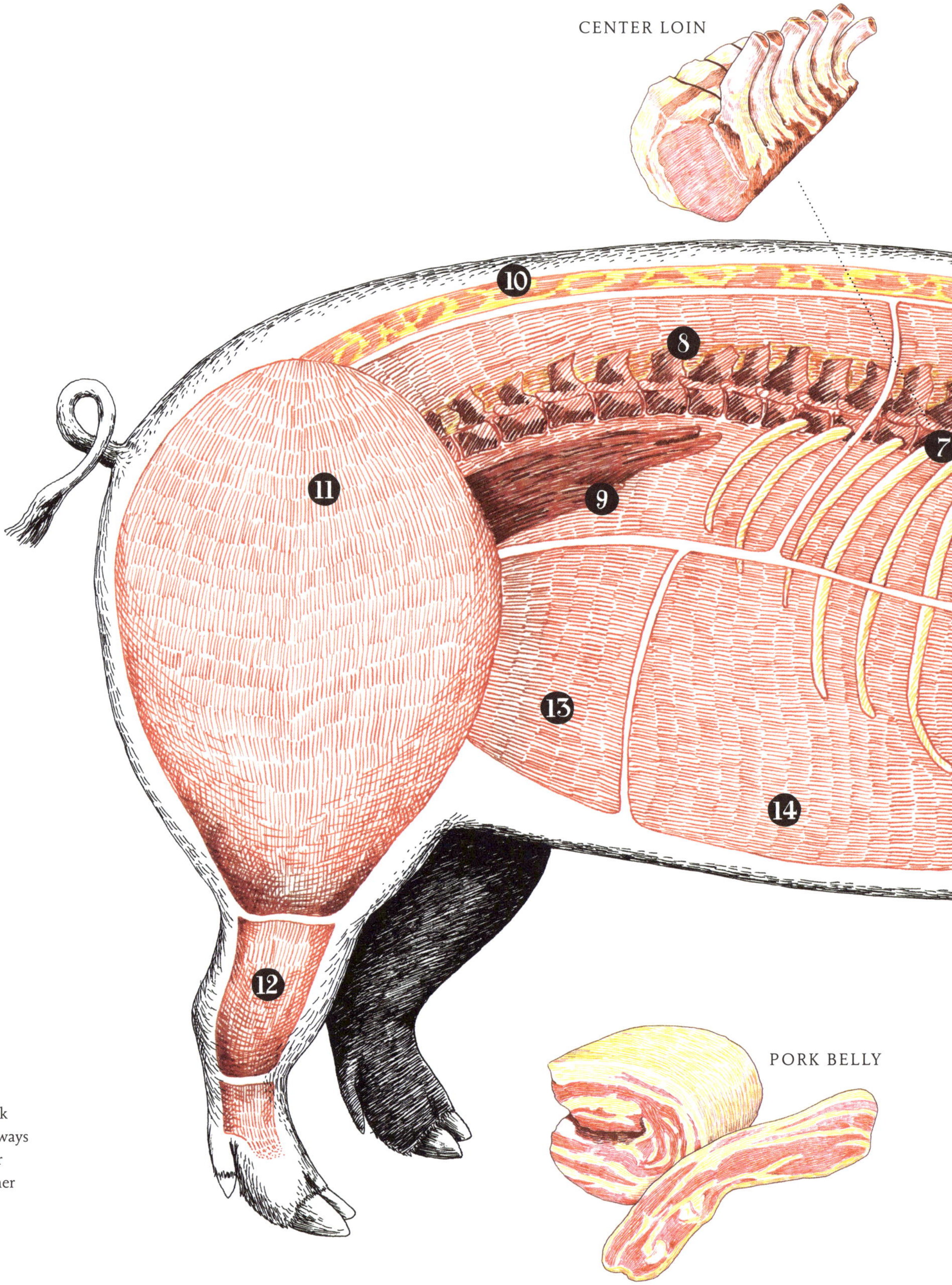

Translator's note
The meat diagram is specific to Dierendonck and the cuts are not always equivalent to British or North American butcher cuts, which also differ by country and region.

DIERENDONCK

PLUMA

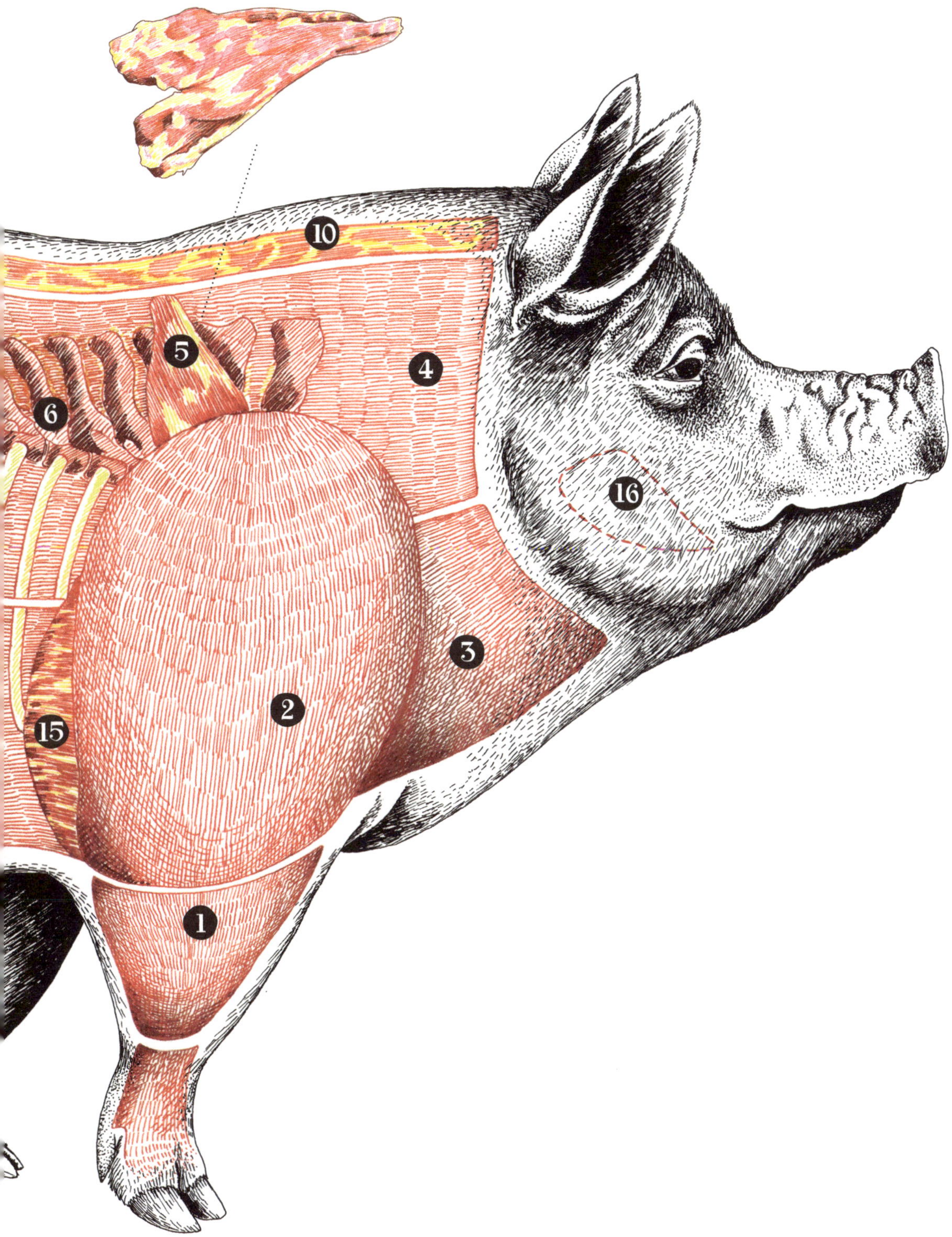

FORE HOCK **1**
HAM SHOULDER **2**
COLLAR BACON **3**
BLADE SHOULDER **4**
PLUMA **5**
BACK RIBS **6**
CENTRE LOIN **7**
LOIN ROAST **8**
PORK TENDERLOIN **9**
FATBACK **10**
HAM **11**
REAR HOCK **12**
BELLY BACON **13**
RIB BACON **14**
SECRETO **15**
CHEEK **16**

STUFFED SUCKLING PIG

"When I was little, customers would order a suckling pig for Christmas or for the village fair. A pig of about ten kilos, with a nice edge of fat, and fed on its mother's milk. Because the customers didn't have an oven at home that was big enough, we did that part too. We roasted it whole. I loved watching my father while he attended to this. I always looked closely at how he worked: the pig was first boned very carefully, so that it was unscathed, then the minced meat, mushrooms, truffles, pistachios, Armagnac and pieces of lean meat followed. And then I watched him stuff and roast the pig. The whole butcher's shop smelled of pork. It would take two, two and a half hours, depending on the weight of the pig and the stuffing.

"We also always roasted a pig on a spit during the evening markets in the summer. I remember how the whole street would come and watch, and taste. The pig was on the spit already turning from early in the morning. When roasting on a spit, make sure it's cooked perfectly on the inside, and the crackling is nice and crispy. You have to stay with it all the time. Baste continuously with the oil and marinade. And then, at some point, it's done. You bite into it and the combination of fatty and tender flesh melts on your tongue. The party can begin. You suddenly find yourself in a Bruegel painting."

BONING, STUFFING AND TRUSSING A SUCKLING PIG

1. Lay the suckling pig on its back.
2. Carefully cut along the ribs down the sternum, on both sides.
3. Score deeper and deeper with the tip of the knife. Carve out the pork loin and make sure to cut loose all the bones. Cut through the atlas (upper cervical vertebra).
4. This allows you to pull the sternum and spine out of the carcass with relative ease. Remove the remaining bones.
5. Now sew up the piglet with sliding knots. Use a trussing needle and butcher's thread. Start at the top. Always pull the thread taut, so that the knots are securely fastened. Sew it closed all the way to its bum.
6. Fill with the forcemeat (see p. 173), pressing it firmly into place. Now sew it shut. Shape the pig so that the stuffing is evenly distributed.

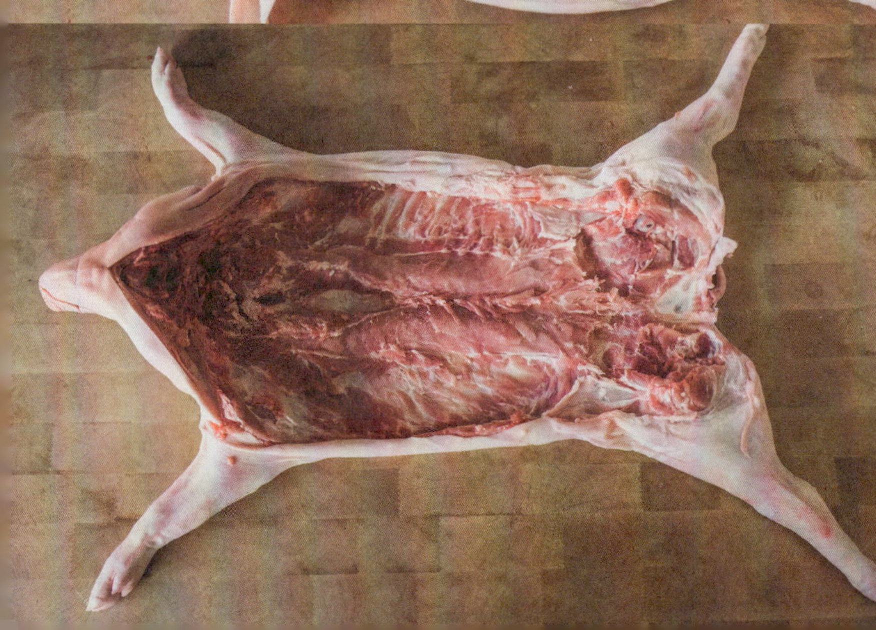

1

2

4
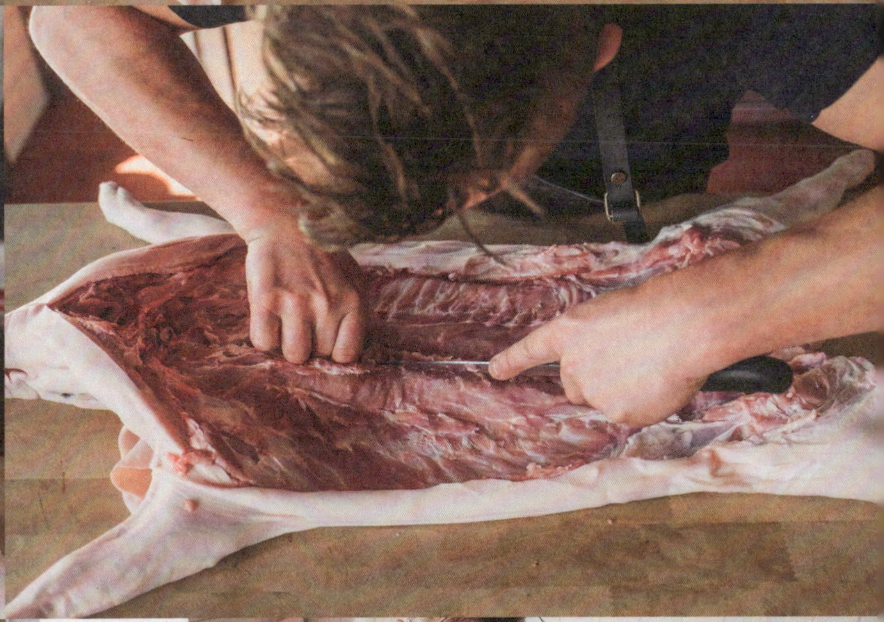

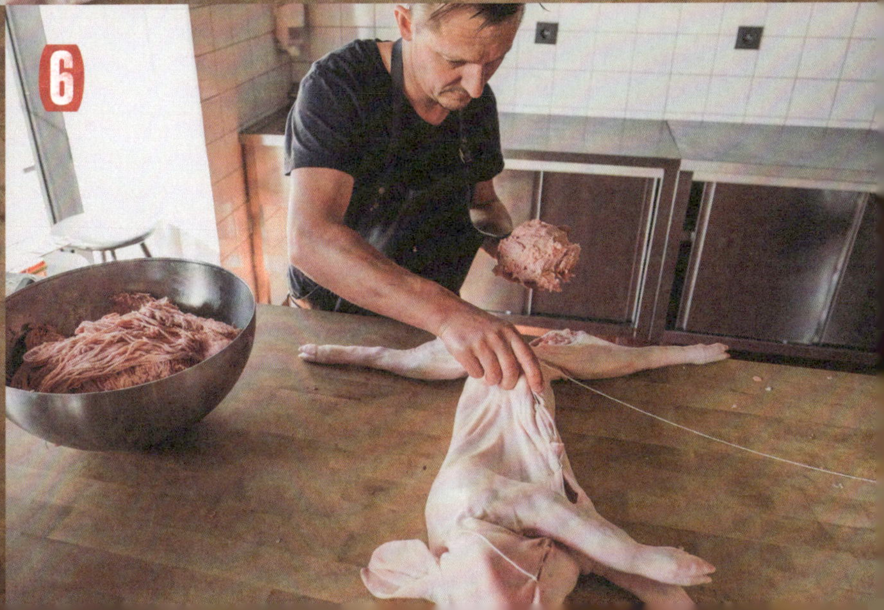
6

STUFFED SUCKLING PIG

FOR A PARTY WITH YOUR FRIENDS

6 H

20 P

1 boned and trussed suckling pig (6 kg / 13 lb 4 oz)
olive oil
freshly ground pepper
coarse sea salt
4 shallots
4 garlic cloves
5 carrots
5 potatoes
500 g (1 lb 2 oz) butter
thyme
bay leaf
rosemary
extra vegetables of the season: for example, a bunch of turnips
2 parsnips
1 butternut squash

Forcemeat

3 kg (6 lb 10 oz) veal and pork mince
5 shallots
300 g (10.5 oz) cream
Armagnac
parsley
4 garlic cloves
400 g (14 oz) mushrooms
salt and pepper
nutmeg
extra spices of your choice: cayenne pepper, for example
optional: some truffle or chestnut purée

Equipment

large roasting pan
trussing needle and thread

Start by making the forcemeat. Peel and finely chop the shallots and sauté them in a knob of butter. Finely chop the mushrooms, add to the shallots and fry briefly. Mix the minced meat with the sautéed shallots, mushrooms, cream and chopped parsley. Add the pressed garlic. Season with Armagnac, pepper, salt, nutmeg and spices of your choice. Adding truffle or chestnut purée is optional.

Stuff the suckling pig with the forcemeat. Take a portion of forcemeat in your hand and press it in firmly. Note: make sure there are no air pockets left anywhere. Sew the pig completely closed. Shape the pig by hand so that the minced meat is evenly distributed throughout.

Rub the roasting pan with olive oil and place the stuffed pig into the pan.

Wash the vegetables and potatoes and chop into rough chunks. Cut the shallots into quarters and crush the garlic. Place the carrots, garlic, shallots and any other vegetables around the pig. Season with pepper and coarse sea salt. Scatter cubes of butter over the vegetables along with the rosemary, thyme and bay leaf.

Preheat the oven to 90°C (195°F) and bake the pig for 4 hours. Spoon the juices over the pig (basting) every half hour. After 2 hours, add the potatoes. After 4 hours, increase the temperature to 150°C (300°F) and continue cooking for an hour or two. Continue to baste the pig regularly with its gravy and check the core temperature of the pig. When it reaches 67°C (150°F), the pig is ready. Remove from the oven, place on the table and carve.

Delicious served with extra mustard and bread.

Tip: *if the suckling pig is drying out in the oven, then cover it with aluminium foil.*

For some extra sauce with the pig: *simply strain the gravy from your roasting pan through a fine sieve. This will be full of the flavours of olive oil, fresh herbs and the piglet, for extra zest.*

SUCKLING PIG À LA ESPAGNOLE

48 H

10-12 P

Roughly crush the cloves. Cut the chilli peppers in half and remove the seeds. Rub the pig with the limes and lime juice and place in a roasting pan. Generously scatter the fresh herbs and coarse sea salt over the pig, then drizzle with olive oil. Cover with foil and leave to rest overnight in the fridge.

Preheat the oven to 90°C (195°F).
Remove the foil. Place the roasting pan in the oven for 8–9 hours until the meat is so tender it falls apart.

Remove from the oven. Remove the bones that separate easily from the meat and the aromatics. What's left are two half pigs without even a single bone. Carefully fold them together.

Place the entire pig neatly in a terrine, gently pressing it in so that there are no air pockets. Pour on the warm gelatinous sauce, which will serve to hold it together when it's unmoulded. Cover tightly with foil. Now place a weight on top of the terrine, to keep it well pressed down and to get rid of any air. Store in the fridge overnight.

Carefully take out of the terrine and cut into thick slices. The structure of the piglet will be nicely visible in your terrine. You can eat it cold as it is, or fry it briefly in a pan or on a barbecue until nicely crispy, both the meat and the skin.

This piglet tastes superb!

1 suckling pig (7–8 kg /c. 16 lb, origin: Spanish Pyrénées)
fresh bay leaf
5 limes
coarse sea salt
peppercorns
5 garlic cloves
2 chilli peppers
fresh rosemary
piment d'Espelette to taste
olive oil
8 shallots

Equipment
large terrine
oven roasting pan

Tip: *ask your butcher to butterfly the suckling pig and leave the skin on.*

PIG ON A SPIT

24 H

75-100 P

1 pig (75 kg / 165 lb)

12° Baumé brine
10 litres (17½ pints) vegetable stock (see p. 243)
1.44 kg (3 lb 3 oz) nitrite brine salt

Marinade
1 litre (35 fl oz) olive oil
1 dark regional beer
250 g (9 oz) pork rub
250 g (9 oz) herbs de provence

Pork rub
100 g (3.5 oz) sea salt
120 g (4 oz) brown sugar
25 g (2 tbsp) fennel seeds
25 g (2 tbsp) black peppercorns
10 g (2 tsp) fresh sage
10 g (2 tsp) fresh rosemary
25 g (2 tbsp) garlic cloves
a pinch of cayenne

Equipment
saw
big knife
brine syringe
spit
brush
trussing needle and 1.5 m (5 ft) of stainless steel wire
a few wheelbarrows of wood

Mix the olive oil with the craft beer, the pork rub and the herbs de provence and let this mixture rest overnight.

Mix everything for the brine (see p. 243), put it into the brine syringe and inject the pig in several places.

Put the pig on the spit. Work the needle and thread along the spine around the spit the full length of the pig, so that the pig is properly trussed.

Arrange the fire under the pig and make sure it is mainly concentrated under the rump and shoulders. The shoulders and hams are the thickest parts, after all. Rotate continually for 10–12 hours, periodically rubbing the marinade into the pork with a brush.

Tip: *keep the fire under control and make sure that the flames do not get too high. If the flames flare up, the fat and the rest of the pig will catch fire.*

Order of carving: shoulders, jowl, pork belly, back meat and pork loins, hams (you need at least two people to do this).

If the meat is not yet fully cooked, give it another quick grill on the barbecue.

PORK RUB
Time: 15 minutes – Quantity: to taste
Mix everything well. Spread it out and let it dry.
Store in a dry cool place.

ELEMENT

PULLED PORK BURGER

11 H

1 P

Glaze
100 ml (3.5 fl oz) soy sauce
200 ml (7 fl oz) acacia honey
50 ml (1.7 fl oz) sushi vinegar
juice of 2 limes
10 ml (2 tsp) yuzu
1 lemongrass stalk
2 cloves of garlic
5 sprigs of thyme
a small piece of ginger
25 ml (0.9 fl oz) ginger syrup
3 star anise
50 g (1.8 oz) Sirop de Liège

60 g (2 oz) pulled pork of Menapian pig
30 g (1 oz) glaze
1 small hamburger bun
2 skinned and deseeded tomatoes
a large pinch of salt
2 tsp of sugar
2 sprigs of thyme
2 cloves of garlic
1 tbsp olive oil
1 red onion
some rocket leaves

Place all the ingredients for the glaze in a saucepan, bring to the boil and simmer for 2 hours.
Strain and reduce until the glaze becomes thick and syrupy.

Heat the meat in the glaze.

Place the tomatoes on a baking sheet lined with baking parchment. Sprinkle the salt, sugar, thyme, garlic and olive oil over the tomatoes and leave to dry out for 9 hours at 80°C (175°F).

Finely slice the red onion.

Arrange everything on a bun and garnish with the petit basque cheese cream and rocket leaves.

Petit basque cheese cream
500 g (1 lb 2 oz) petit basque cheese
1 litre (35 fl oz) milk
14 g (0.5 oz) kappa (Texturas)
4 tbsp good olive oil
salt

CHEESE CREAM (this is the basic recipe for all cheese creams)
Cut the cheese into small dice and bring to the boil with the milk and the kappa. Remember to stir well as the mixture can catch easily. Pour the liquid cream on to a sheet and let it set and harden (this should take about 10 minutes). Transfer the cheese to a mixer and mix until smooth. Add the olive oil and season to taste with salt.

SHORT RIBS OF MENAPIAN PIG

WITH SOUR CREAM AND CHICKPEAS

3 H

2 P

Place all the ingredients for the glaze in a saucepan, bring to the boil and simmer for 2 hours.
Strain and reduce until the glaze becomes thick and syrupy.

Grill or fry the short ribs.

Mix the sour cream with the lime juice, olive oil and za'atar, and season with salt and pepper.

Glaze the short ribs and serve with the sour cream and chickpeas.

Garnish with the basil cress.

Glaze

100 ml (3.5 fl oz) soy sauce
200 ml (7 fl oz) acacia honey
50 ml (1.7 fl oz) sushi vinegar
juice of 2 limes
10 ml (2 tsp) yuzu
1 lemongrass stalk
2 cloves of garlic
5 sprigs of thyme
a small piece of ginger
25 ml (0.9 fl oz) ginger syrup
3 star anise
50 g (1.8 oz) Sirop de Liège

2 pre-cooked short ribs
300 g (10.5 oz) sour cream
juice of 1 lime
3 tbsp good olive oil
a large pinch of za'atar
salt and pepper
1 tin of chickpeas
basil cress

CRISPY PIG'S EARS

WITH HOT KETCHUP

6 H

6 P

4 pig's ears
fleur de sel
lemon zest

Stock for the pig's ears
2 onions
½ leek
2 celery stalks
12 peppercorns
a large pinch of salt
1 bulb of garlic
2 carrots
8 sprigs of thyme
3 bay leaves

Hot ketchup
1 kg (2 lb 4 oz) san marzano tomatoes
250 g (9 oz) red onions
250 g (9 oz) dessert apples
22.5 g (0.8 oz) smoked salt (Maldon)
250 g (9 oz) brown sugar
15 g (0.5 oz) smoked paprika
250 ml (9 fl oz) apple vinegar
100 ml (3.5 fl oz) apple juice

Cover the pig's ears and the ingredients for the stock with water, bring to the boil and simmer gently (for approximately 4 hours) until the ears are tender – test for tenderness with a knife.

Remove the ears from the stock and leave to cool for 2 hours. Cut into thin strips, about 0.5 cm (¼ in) thick, and fry at 180°C (350°F) until crispy. Be careful as pig's ears tend to spatter! Place the strips on kitchen paper and sprinkle with the fleur de sel and lemon zest.

Stew the tomatoes, onions, apples and salt in a large pan. Add the sugar and smoked paprika, continue to cook and then deglaze with the apple vinegar and apple juice. Simmer until all the ingredients are nicely cooked, mix well and strain through a fine sieve.

Serve the ears on baking parchment, with the hot ketchup on the side.

SALAMI PURE PORC

24 H
PREPARATION

3 W
RIPENING

5 KG
11 LB

2 kg (4 lb 6 oz) lean pork
2 kg (4 lb 6 oz) fatty pork belly
100 g (3.5 oz) sodium nitrite
12 g (1 tbsp) brown sugar
500 g (1 lb 1 oz) salami leftovers
12 g (1 tbsp) whole white pepper
8 g (1½ tsp) ground white pepper
2 g (½ tsp) cardamom
120 ml (4 fl oz) dry white wine
2 garlic cloves, finely chopped with a dash of white wine
thick pig-intestine casings (diameter 40 mm / 1½ in)

Equipment
sausage stuffer machine
meat grinder

Put the meat in the freezer for 1–2 hours – until it's cold but not frozen. Grind it finely through the 5-mm plate on the meat grinder, together with the salami leftovers (we call this salami *entwurst;* it gives the cure a good start). Mix with the spices, brown sugar, brine salt and white wine.

Fill the large pig-intestine casings very carefully with the cold dough, it is important that this is kept chilled to prevent smearing.

Portion the salami to your preferred length and hang it for 2 days in 18–22°C (64-68°F) with a humidity level of 95%. Wash off the white mould with cold water and continue drying.

Dry for another 21 days in 18–22°C (64-68°F) with 80% humidity. You can hang the salami to dry for as long as you want, but keep checking to make sure that the outside doesn't dry out. This is called "case hardening", meaning it forms a dry crust that will not allow the moisture inside to get out, so it will stop the salami from drying.

Tip: *if you don't have a curing chamber, place the salami in a container, cover with a wet towel and place in a warm, draught-free cellar.*

H

“You can tell the quality of a butcher by his minced meat. That is why, as a butcher’s son, you start learning to make it when you’re ten or 11 years old. More often than not, this is your first step in your career: your father’s entrusting you with the first of his trade secrets, and because you’re working with the less expensive cuts, you’re allowed to experiment. Not too much, though, because your work is going to be judged seriously. A good butcher must know his breeders, he can appreciate a beautiful animal, knows how to carve meat and make a neat shop window, but you can recognise a real craftsman by his small preparations. His pressed head, his pâté, his black pudding, that sort of thing. Every *charcutier* has his secrets. No two black puddings are alike; everyone makes theirs their own way. The same for minced meat. There is no simpler thing – and that is why that’s where you often recognise the hand of the master, the DNA of a butcher’s shop. A craftsman is just as demanding of the quality of his minced meat as he is of his best steak.

“My minced meat is a tribute to my father. He is retired, but still comes to the shop every day. He tastes, gives his opinion, talks to the customers. He’s a bit like the temple guard. And he watches over the minced meat, keeping a close eye on how we cut, how we chop. The first thing he taught me is how to bone a shoulder and a pork belly, and how to hold my knife… That is the foundation of our minced meat. We cut thick. We prefer a fairly fatty, well-structured cut of meat. Fat that melts in the mouth. We judge by eye the right mixture of belly and shoulder meat: it depends on the pig. The meat of every animal is different and minced meat is not an exact science. Sometimes you put in a little more pork belly – that meat is fatter than the shoulder – sometimes a little less. Then add the spices: salt, nutmeg, cardamom, mace… And eggs. One egg per kilo. The spices shouldn’t dominate. It’s the meat you want to taste. That is the basic rule with us: it is the meat that gives flavour to our minced meat. The tendons should also be neatly trimmed from the shoulders, otherwise you’d find them in the minced meat. And then there are the blades of your meat mill: without a good cutting blade, there is no good mincemeat. Simple isn’t always easy…”

BONING A PIG'S HEAD

Turn the head over.

Remove the lower jawbone.

Separate the snout from the nasal bone.

Break off this bone just before the eye socket.

Break the remaining bone in two where it is level with the brain cavity.

Finally, remove the eye and the tough part behind the ear.

Arrange the head nicely on a wooden board.

BRAWN TO SHARE

MY NEW TAKE ON 'COCHON DE LUXE'

24 H

4-6 P

8 litres (14 pints) water
2 half pig heads
576 g (20 oz) sodium nitrite
6 litres (10½ pints) vegetable stock (see p. 243)
4 carrots
4 celery stalks
thyme
bay leaf
pickled vegetables
parsley
mustard
bread

Equipment
large board

Soak the heads overnight in a light 6° Baumé brining solution (see p. 243).
Remove the heads from the brine and place them in a cooking pot.
Cover with the stock and add the coarsely chopped carrot and celery, bay leaf and thyme.
Bring to a boil and let it simmer on a low heat for 3–4 hours.

Tip: *the meat is done when you can easily push through the skin with your thumb.*
Remove the heads from the stock and remove the bones (see p. 198).
Arrange on a nice wooden board and serve with bread, mustard, fresh parsley and pickled vegetables of your choice (see p. 242).

H

“The brawn I like looks very different from the jelly terrine you usually find at the butcher's. It's a dream come true for me to put half a pig's head on the table and share it with friends. It's best eaten with your fingers, a slice of rustic bread, mustard and pickles. A picnic at home. It makes an impression, but it's not that complicated. You order a pig's head from the butcher. That is where you'll be able to tell whether you're dealing with a professional. If he listens to you with interest, he is a butcher with heart for his craft. Ask him to clean the pig's head. The ears must be removed, and the skin must be cleaned. Then you just have to let it cook gently in a vegetable stock. The secret of the recipe is, as always, take your time. Two hours, two and a half hours, three hours… The meat should be tender and fall off the bone.

“Take the pig's head out of the stock and let it drain and cool. Then remove the bones and jaw. The only things you don't eat from a pig's head are the bones and the eyes. Everything else tastes good. Then you break the cartilage. Very easy. Toasted farmhouse bread, a selection of chutneys and let the party begin. It may be less obvious than a bowl of peeled carrots, but it is an experience!”

BOSKA

'LA FÊTE DU COCHON'

48 H

4 P

6 pork cheeks
2 black pudding sausages from your butcher (approx. 400 g / 14 oz)
1 block of 400 g (14 oz) fat salted bacon
2 litres (3½ pints) vegetable stock (see p. 243)
acacia honey
farm butter
fresh thyme
pickled vegetables of your choice (see p. 242)
balsamic vinegar
2 litres (3½ pints) water
144 g (5 oz) sodium nitrite

Make a light 6° Baumé brine with the water and sodium nitrite (see p. 243), then leave the pork cheeks to soak in the brine overnight.

Remove the pork cheeks from the brine and place in a cooking pot with the bacon. Cover with vegetable stock, bring to a boil and simmer for 3–4 hours on a low heat until the meat is completely tender.

Turn off the heat and let the meat steep in the stock overnight.

Remove the meat and cut the bacon into pieces.

Fry the black pudding in a knob of butter.

In another pan, fry the bacon and pork cheeks.

Add the honey and caramelise the bacon and cheeks.

Carve the pork cheeks and black pudding into slices.

Deglaze the pork cheek pan with a dash of balsamic vinegar and reduce slightly. If necessary, add some more honey to achieve the flavour you want.

Dress a plate with the pork cheeks, bacon and black pudding. Scatter the pickled vegetables and fresh thyme over the meat.

Garnish with some swirls of balsamic syrup.

BLACK PUDDING

I LEARNED TO MAKE THIS FROM THE BRUSSELEIRS

5 H PREPARATION

24 H RESTING

5 KG 11 LB

Check the collar bacon for glands, blood elements and rind. Remove these if you find them, as they will give the black pudding an unpleasant taste.

Peel and finely chop the onions and fry them gently in some olive oil. Make sure they are soft, otherwise they'll give your black pudding an unpleasant texture.

Finely grind the brawn with the collar and back bacon, then mix with the warm sautéed onion and apple compote until it comes together in an evenly mixed, doughy paste. Now heat the blood in the bain-marie, stirring gently to keep it from getting too thick.

Once it's warm, gently add all the other ingredients including the spices. Add the cream at the very end.

Sometimes it's best to taste again at this stage to see if you need more salt and pepper. Carefully pull a casing over the sausage maker or funnel, and tie it securely. Carefully fill each casing with the black pudding and portion to your preferred length.

Gently bring a pot of water or vegetable stock to a boil. As soon as the water is boiling, you can put the black pudding into the water and poach gently at 80°C (175°F) for 30–35 minutes. To see if the black pudding is cooked through, prick it with a needle. If no blood runs out, the sausage is cooked. It's important to cool the black pudding as quickly as possible in iced water, so that the sausage retains a nice colour, and to prevent it from drying out.

1.5 kg (3 lb 5 oz) onion
1.5 litres (53 fl oz) fresh pig's blood
500 g (1 lb 2 oz) fine brawn
500 g (1 lb 2 oz) back bacon
500 g (1 lb 2 oz) collar bacon
200 ml (7 fl oz) cream
200 ml (7 fl oz) fresh apple compote

pig-intestine casings
(diameter 39–40 mm / 1½ in)

Spices
36 g (1.2 oz) table salt
9 g (2 tsp) black pepper
1.2 g (¼ tsp) nutmeg
1 ground clove
4.5 g (1 tsp) allspice
45 g (1.6 oz) cane sugar

Equipment
meat grinder or food processor
large pot
sausage maker or funnel
bain-marie

Tip: cut open a fresh warm black pudding and spread it on toast – success guaranteed!

TRADITIONAL BLOOD PUDDING

WITH PEPERKOEK (SPICED BREAD) AND TOAST

1H

4P

1 black pudding
small loaf of wholemeal bread

Peperkoek cream
500 g (1 lb 2 oz) peperkoek (without honey)
100 g (3.5 oz) butter
300 ml (10 fl oz) milk
a pinch of salt
lime zest

Miso cream
basic mayonnaise (see p. 243) without salt
1 tbsp miso paste

Slice the black pudding into equal segments and fry until crisp.

Cut the bread into slices of ± 1 cm (½ in), punch out small circles and fry in butter until crisp.

Place all the ingredients for the peperkoek cream into a blender or mixer bowl, except for the milk. Warm the milk slightly, then add it too and mix to a smooth cream. Transfer to a piping bag and chill in the fridge.

Place all the ingredients for the miso cream into the blender, except for the grapeseed oil. Combine, then add the grapeseed oil.

Arrange the black pudding on the toast and plate up.

1
2
3
4
5
Dierendonck

LINKING WHITE SAUSAGES

1 Fill the intestine neatly and evenly.

2 Knot the ends closed and lay out the entire sausage in two rows, side by side. Link a sausage in each row. Then twist both sausages together. Repeat these steps to create two more sausages.

3 Now take the end of the first row and pull it through the opening made by the second pair of sausages. Do the same with the other row. Make a sausage in each row for a third time. Twist into a link.

4 Take the ends of each row and pull through the loop again.

5 Repeat these steps until the sausage is completely linked.

SPICED WHITE PUDDING

HENDRIK'S OWN VERSION OF THE MÜNCHNER WEISSWURST

24 H

5 KG
11 LB

Put the back bacon, the veal fricassee and the pork meat in the freezer for 1–2 hours, so that it is cold but not frozen. Mix the fricassee with the pork, eggs, cream, table salt, half the milk and half the ice in the cutter at 2°C (35°F).

Remove from the processor.

Mix the bacon with the rest of the milk and the ice at 8°C (45°F). Slowly add the chopped meat to the back bacon. Process up to 14°C (55°F).

Add all the spices, vegetables, minced meat and brawn and mix to the desired fineness.

Transfer to the sausage stuffer and carefully fill the casings. Portion the sausages to your preferred length. Poach in water for 35 minutes at about 75°C (165°F). Important: don't let the water boil.

Cool the sausages immediately in iced water and let them rest overnight in the fridge under a towel.

1.5 kg (3 lb 5 oz) ground back bacon
750 g (1 lb 10.5 oz) ground veal fricassee
750 g (1 lb 10.5 oz) ground lean pork
500 g (1 lb 2 oz) ice shavings
300 g (10.5 oz) whole milk (frozen)
half a leek
1 small onion
200 g (7 oz) brawn
100 g (3.5 oz) apple compote
2 farm eggs
75 ml (2.5 fl oz) cream
300 g (10.5 oz) coarsely minced pork
1 bunch fresh parsley
75 g (2.5 oz) sea salt
2 g (½ tsp) cardamom
4 g (1 tsp) freshly ground pepper
2 g (½ tsp) mace
2 g (½ tsp) ginger
4 g (1 tsp) lime juice

pig-intestine casings
(diameter 40 mm+ / 1½ in+)

***Tip:** the Münchner Weisswurst is extra light thanks to the processing method. The meat is processed once, and then processed again with the fat. This ensures an airy mixture that is not too heavy on the stomach and that fries up nicely in the pan.*

WHITE PUDDING

WITH FLAMBÉED APPLE COMPOTE

EXTRA TASTY

0.5 H

4 P

4 white sausages
2 kg (4 lb 7 oz) cooking apples
50 g (2 oz) fine sugar
100 g (3.5 oz) butter
calvados
thyme

Peel the apples and cut them into pieces.
Melt the butter and sauté the apples.
Add the sugar and caramelise briefly.
Flambé with calvados – don't forget to turn off the extractor fan!
Make sure the apples still have some bite to them.
Melt some butter in a pan over a low heat.
Fry the sausages until crispy on the outside and warmed through on the inside.
Serve with the apples and garnish with fresh thyme.

H

"There is nothing complicated about sausages. With black pudding, there must be a proper balance between four ingredients: pig's blood, fat, brawn and onions. The rest depends on the quality of the pig and is a matter of taste. Which fat do you want to use? Because each type of fat brings its own different set of qualities. Also, the blood must be fresh. Then add pepper, raisins, apples and anything else you want. There are as many types of sausage as there are *charcutiers.*

"For white pudding, you use lean white meat: veal, chicken or pork. You add fat, cream, butter or pork fat, eggs and milk. You put all the ingredients in the food processor. Season the mixture to taste and make sure that it has a fine texture. This is important. My white pudding resembles the Münchner Weisswurst, a light German sausage. The Munich butchers use only veal. To be able to call it sausage, there must also be pork in it. For the fat I use coarsely minced pork and a little bit of brawn. Onions, milk, spices. And then the emulsion. But white sausages should be eaten warm! Remove them from the refrigerator two hours before cooking. You fry them quickly in a frying pan or *a la plancha.* Eat with a slice of farmhouse bread... Delicious!"

WHITE PUDDING CARCASSE

WITH FREGOLA, THYME AND A TARRAGON CREAM

1 H

2 P

Fry the white pudding.

Combine the cream, water, sherry vinegar, thyme leaves and some salt and pepper in a small saucepan, bring to the boil and whisk in loads of butter until you get a lovely, thick sauce.

Prepare the fregola with all the ingredients.

Place all the ingredients for the tarragon mayonnaise in a mixer, then add the grapeseed oil.

Spoon the fregola on to the white pudding, add some dots of tarragon mayonnaise, garnish with lemon zest and finish with grated parmesan cheese and lime cress. Serve with the thyme sauce.

1 white pudding
lemon zest
piece of parmesan cheese
lime cress

Thyme sauce
100 ml (3.5 fl oz) cream
some water
2 tbsp sherry vinegar
salt and pepper
10 sprigs of thyme, leaves finely chopped
butter (loads!)

30 g (1 oz) fregola
chives
tarragon
1 tsp chardonnay vinegar
1 tsp sushi vinegar
salt and pepper
lemon zest
2 tsp olive oil

Tarragon mayonnaise
basic mayonnaise (see p. 243)
1 bunch of tarragon, leaves finely chopped

“This is the biggest classic in our range. It is very pure and simple, but there was nothing my father paid more attention to than making sure I could make this the exact way he wanted it – right down to the last detail. The pork collar must be trimmed and chopped, the liver ground just so, and everything is blended in the *pétrin* [kneading trough] so that it is mixed very well by hand. This is the mother of all our pâtés, the basis for Normandy pâté, pheasant and hare pâté and so on. It is an honour for me to make this pâté; I inherited our pride in it from my father. And every morning, when we sit at the table after a few hours' work and eat some of this pâté on bread, my father says: 'That's good pâté, isn't it!' I hope to hear him say that many, many more times. *Merci, Papa!*”

GRANDMOTHER'S PÂTÉ

BY RAYMOND DIERENDONCK

24 H

2 KG
4 LB 8 OZ

1.1 kg (2 lb 6 oz) pork liver
1 kg (2 lb 4 oz) pork collar
1 egg
70 g (2.5 oz) onion
30 g (1 oz) sodium nitrite
6 g (1½ tsp) pepper
4 g (1 tsp) vanilla sugar
500 g (1 lb 2 oz) back bacon
300 g (10 oz) pork caul
vegetable stock (see p. 243)

Equipment
powerful food processor or meat grinder
terrine, 2 kg (4 lb 7 oz) capacity

Carefully remove the bile ducts from the liver, because they give a bitter-sour taste to the pâté. Remove glands, bloody elements and any irregularities from the pork collar, then cut into 5 cm x 5 cm (2 in x 2 in) cubes.

Cook the cubes in the stock at 105°C (220°F) until the meat is completely tender. You'll know it's done when you can push through the fat easily. While the collar is cooking, grind the liver with the egg and raw onion, fairly coarsely – use the 5-mm plate on the meat grinder.

Mix in the pepper, vanilla sugar and sodium nitrite.

When the pork collar is cooked enough, put it through the grinder too. Mix everything together to a smooth, evenly mixed consistency. Place the back bacon at the bottom of the terrine, then fill the dish firmly with the liver and collar mixture so that there are no air pockets. Cover with the rinsed pork caul.

Bake the pâté very carefully at 85°C (185°F) until the core temperature has reached 67°C (150°F). *(We've been practising low-heat baking since I was a kid!)* This slow bake produces a very tasty and creamy pâté.

***Tip:** ask your butcher for some sodium nitrite, so that the pâté retains its colour. If you work with normal curing salt, your pâté will have a slightly grey cast. The vanilla sugar is used to offset the bitterness of the liver.*

H

“Rillette in a terrine is something to eat with friends. On grilled farmhouse bread or a fresh baguette with pickles. The perfect appetiser in my opinion. A *déjeuner sur l'herbe*. The secret of rillette is the texture. And the secret of the texture is a hammer…

“A *charcutier* has to respect the texture. We work according to an old French recipe with a mixture of duck and pork that we let confit in the fat for hours. When it is cooked, we remove the fat and flatten the meat with our hands to preserve the texture. If you use a meat grinder, the fibres are lost. The farmers in the French countryside use a fork. My father preferred to use a hammer.

“In the old days, the terrine was made before the winter season, when the pig was slaughtered, and covered with lard to preserve it. So if a friend invites you to a dinner party and you show up with your terrine of rillette, you can be sure it'll be a hit with the other guests; they'll eat until their bellies are round.”

PORK AND DUCK RILLETTE WITH SAGE

24 H

2.5 KG
5 LB 9 OZ

1 duck
1 pork belly top with fat, meat and rind
1 onion
1 garlic clove
1 pork leg (sawn in two)
vegetable stock (see p. 243)
20 g (0.7 oz) sodium nitrite per litre of water
ground pepper
sea salt
nutmeg
40 g (1.4 oz) fresh sage

Equipment
terrine
large cooking pot

Place all the meat in a pot and cover with water. Add 20 g (0.7 oz) of sodium nitrite per litre of water. Steep in the brine overnight. Carefully remove the meat from the brine and place the belly top skin-down at the bottom of a large cooking pot. The skin of the belly will scorch slightly due to the heat and give the dish more flavour. Put the rest of the brined meat on top and cover in vegetable stock.

Bring to a boil and simmer for at least 4 hours on a low heat, until the meat is nice and tender and can be picked off the bone. Remove the cooked meat from the stock. Set aside the stock with the fat.

Pick the meat from the duck, removing bones and any tough pieces. Remove the rind and glands from the pork belly, then mix it with the duck meat.

Beat and pound the meat with a rolling pin until you have a mass of shredded meat, then add the fat from the stock and the duck skins. The pounding is the fun part of making rillette: you can vent a lot of frustration in a few minutes.

When you have achieved the desired consistency, weigh the meat and put it in a saucepan with an equal volume of stock. Add the crushed garlic and finely chopped onion, season with pepper, sea salt, nutmeg and sage to taste.

Let it simmer for another 1.5 hours over a low flame.

Transfer to the terrine and let it cool for at least a night.

This rillette goes perfectly with brown bread and pickled vegetables (see p. 242).

RABBIT DE MOEREN PÂTÉ

WITH A STRONG LOCAL BEER AND PLUMS

24 H

2.5 KG
5 LB 9 OZ

First make the pastry. Mix the sea salt with the flour. Cut the butter and the lard into pea-sized pieces with two knives and add to the flour. Make a well in the centre and pour in some water. Carefully mix everything until the dough comes together – the fat can still be slightly visible.

It's important that you work quickly, so that the dough does not get too warm under your hands. Let it rest for 1 hour in the fridge. Roll out the dough into 2 nice flat sheets.

Remove glands, bloody parts and any irregularities from the pork collar. Also remove the bile ducts from the liver.

Cook the collar in vegetable stock until the meat is completely soft. Grind the liver finely (3 mm) with the egg and raw onion. Then finely grind the soft-boiled collar and mix well with the liver, spices and salt. Open the bottle of local beer. Drink half of it (cheers!) and mix the rest into the rabbit pâté with the plums.

Grease a terrine with some butter or lard and line it with pastry. Make sure the terrine is lined completely. Fill with the pâté. Fold the pastry over to close and brush with egg yolk. Cover with another sheet of pastry. Poke three holes in the top and brush again with egg yolk.

Bake the pie for 15 minutes in a preheated oven at 160°C (320°F). Lower the temperature to 74°C (165°F). Bake to a core temperature of 67°C (152°F). Let it cool for 24 hours before demoulding.

***Tip:** hold the terrine over the fire or heat it in a bain-marie, so that the fat melts and the pie comes loose. Now slice your pie – you will see that the plums give a nice garnish and taste. If you don't have time to make your own pastry, you can use store-bought puff pastry.*

1 kg (2 lb 4 oz) rabbit liver from De Moeren
1.2 kg (2 lb 10 oz) pork collar
200 g (7 oz) dried plums
1 bottle of dark regional beer
1 farm egg
30 g (1 oz) sodium nitrite
7 g (1 tsp) pepper
70 g (2 oz) onion
2 sheets of shortcrust pastry
2 litres (3½ pints) vegetable stock (see p. 243)
2 extra egg yolks
1 knob of farm butter

Shortcrust pastry

1 kg (2 lb 4 oz) flour
20 g (4 tsp) sea salt
250 g (9 oz) lard
200 g (7 oz) butter
500 ml (17 fl oz) cold water

Equipment

terrine, 3 kg (6 lb 10 oz) capacity

H

My mother always told me and my brother Alexander to eat pigeon because it would make us strong. Her pigeons were exquisite, perfectly roasted, a little pink. And yet preparing a pigeon is far from simple. Or, rather, it is simple, but you have to stay focused. My mother fries them in a sauté pan with butter and a chopped shallot. Constantly basting them with the butter. Cooking with us has always been something simple and unpretentious, but it is done with great care. Basting makes the skin crispy, while the juice remains in the meat.

"Make sure the meat stays pink… pink, not *saignant* (bloody). And tender. And that's why you have to baste constantly – really all the time – with the hot butter.

"Each ingredient has its specific character. That creates specific fragrances, but also images that you remember. My mother's recipe is still the best. She greatly influenced my taste. My father was the man of the product, my mother shaped it. I remember how they discussed recipes. And at home we tasted everything and shared our opinions."

PIGEON TERRINE

500 g (1 lb 2 oz) collar bacon
150 g (5 oz) chicken liver
100 g (3.5 oz) duck liver
meat from 4 Steenvoorde pigeons
16 g (3 tsp) sodium nitrite
2 g (½ tsp) freshly ground pepper
1 g (¼ tsp) sugar
1 g (¼ tsp) nutmeg
50 ml (1.7 fl oz) cream
1 farm egg
1 tbsp cognac
1 large shallot
75 ml (2.5 fl oz) Banyuls wine

Extra

1 pork caul
back bacon

Equipment

1 terrine

Bone the pigeons carefully and thoroughly. Set aside the breast fillet for later.

Sauté the finely chopped shallots until they are a nice golden brown, then add the pigeon carcasses and thighs. Season with salt and pepper and fry until everything is nicely crisped. Deglaze with the cognac and the Banyuls wine, allowing it to reduce slightly until the meat is tender.

Take out the bones and neatly pick off the meat. Put the meat in a blender together with the remaining gravy and shallots and combine into a firm mass.

Remove from the blender and mix in the collar bacon and chicken livers. Put the pigeon back in, together with the duck liver, sugar and all the spices, and mix roughly, making sure it is all well blended.

You can now put this in a terrine that is lined with the back bacon. Make sure there are no air pockets!

Bake the terrine at 75°C (165°F) to a core temperature of 67°C (152°F), then leave to cool overnight.

I garnish the terrine with the pigeon breasts that were set aside earlier.

I sauté them briefly until they're pink, and use them to decorate the top of the terrine, or serve them in slices on the plate.

3 U

1 KG
2 LB 4 OZ

LAMB

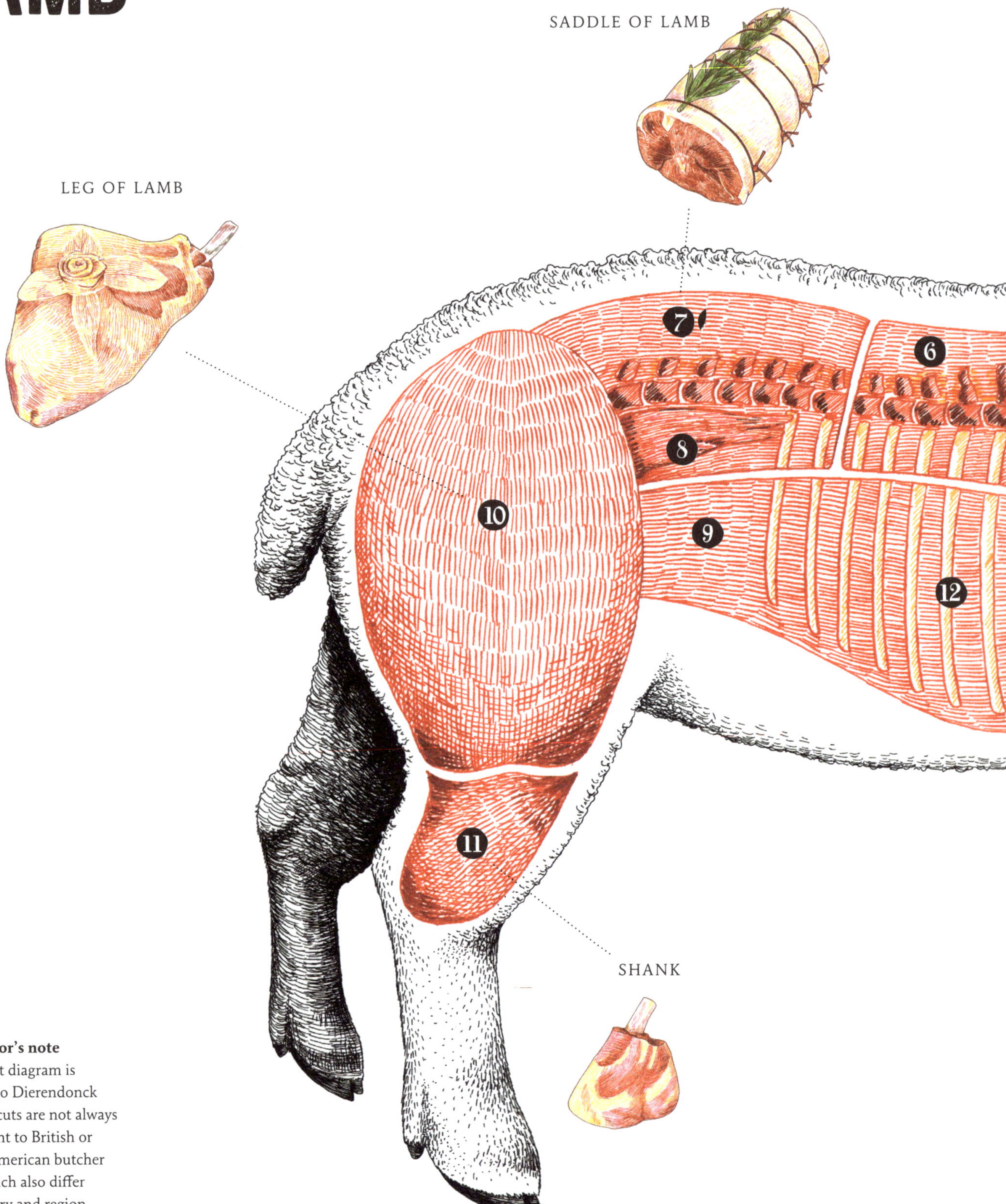

Translator's note
The meat diagram is specific to Dierendonck and the cuts are not always equivalent to British or North American butcher cuts, which also differ by country and region.

DIERENDONCK

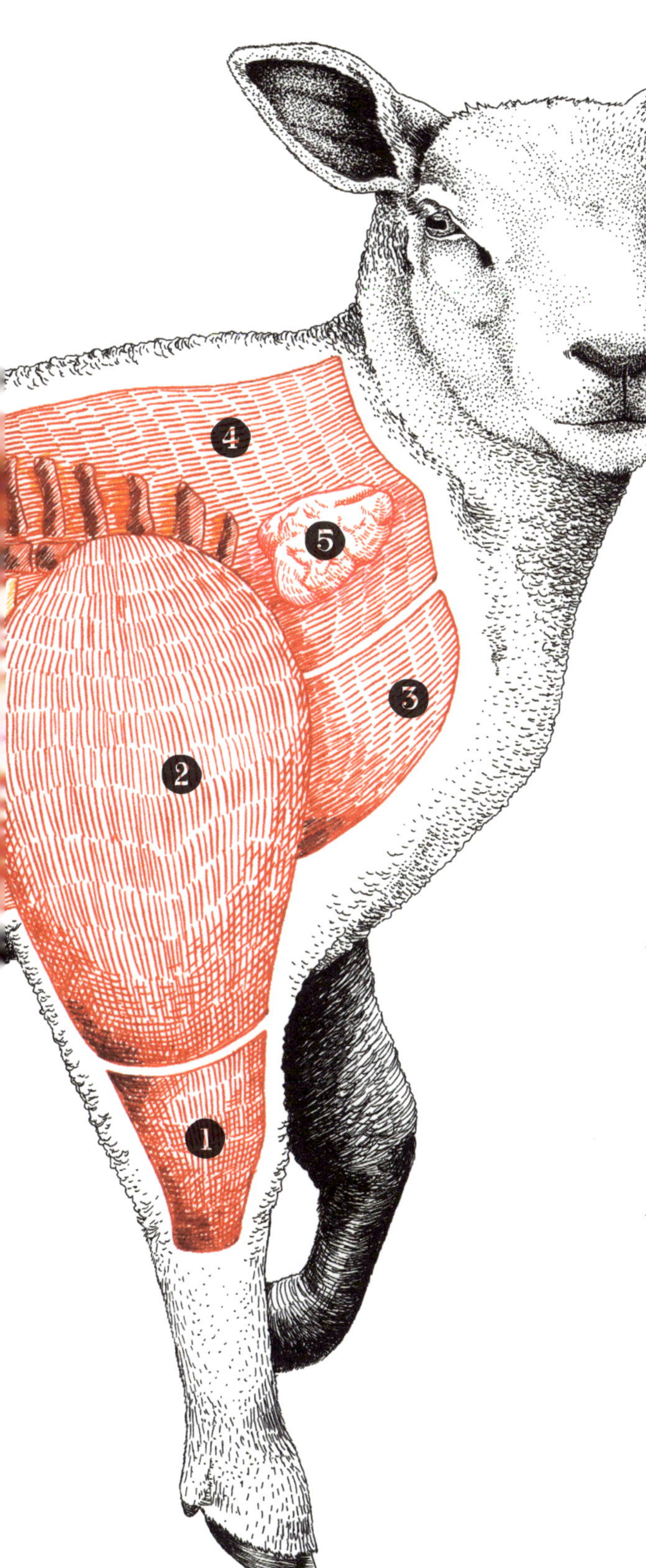

CROWN OF LAMB

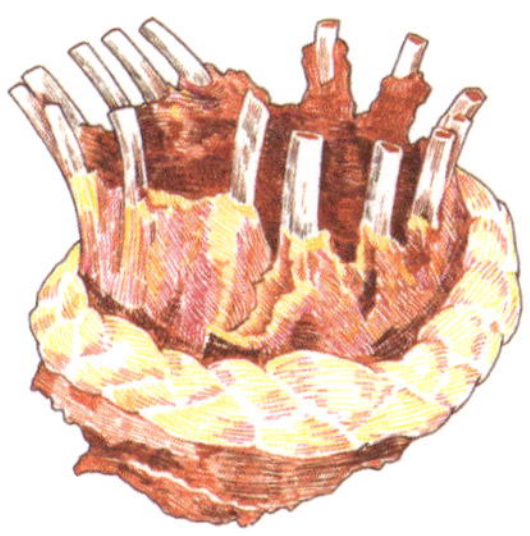

TOURNEDOS OF LAMB

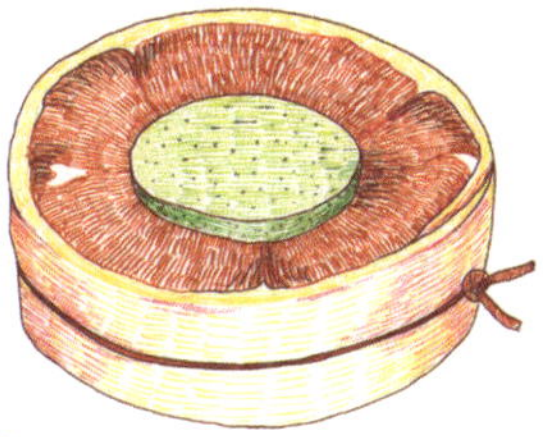

FORE SHANK 1
SHOULDER 2
BREAST 3
NECK 4
LAMB SWEETBREADS 5
LAMB RACK/CHOPS 6
SADDLE 7
LOIN 8
LAMB BELLY 9
LEG OF LAMB 10
REAR SHANK 11
FLANK 12

LAMB SHOULDER FROM THE PYRÉNÉES

MEDITERRANEAN-STYLE

2 H

4 P

750 g (1 lb 10 oz) lamb shoulder from the Pyrénées, bone-in
freshly ground pepper
coarse sea salt
mild olive oil
sage
rosemary
bay leaf
a few cloves of garlic
100 g (3.5 oz) cherry tomatoes
1 courgette
1 fennel
and some extra time…

Lamb rub

100 g (3.5 oz) sea salt
75 g (2.5 oz) brown sugar
25 g (2 tbsp) mustard seeds
25 g (0.9 oz) fennel seeds
25 g (0.9 oz) garlic cloves
10 g (0.3 oz) fresh rosemary
10 g (0.3 oz) fresh thyme
zest of 1 lime
pinch of cumin

Equipment

roasting pan or casserole dish

Place the lamb shoulder in a casserole dish or roasting pan with olive oil, pepper, salt, sage, rosemary, bay leaf and a few roughly crushed garlic cloves. Bake for 2 hours in an oven preheated to 90°C (195°F).

Meanwhile, chop the courgette and fennel into small pieces. After two hours, increase the temperature to 110°C (230°F). Add the fennel, cherry tomatoes and courgette to the pan. Let it cook for another 30 minutes.

Add some extra olive oil if needed.

Remove from the oven when the vegetables are nicely cooked and your lamb shoulder is about to fall apart.

Just put it on the table like this and pull the meat from the bone. Serve with bread.

LAMB RUB

Time: 15 minutes – Quantity: to taste

Mix everything well. Spread it out and let it dry a bit.

Store in a dry cool place

PULLED LAMB BURGER

2.5 H

1 P

Place all the ingredients for the glaze in a saucepan, bring to the boil and simmer for 2 hours.

Strain and reduce until the glaze becomes thick and syrupy.

Heat the pulled lamb with the glaze in a saucepan.

Pull off the sage leaves and deep-fry at 190°C (374°F). Transfer to some kitchen paper and sprinkle with fleur de sel.

Place the meat on the bun and garnish with the black garlic cream and the sage.

Glaze

100 ml (3.5 fl oz) soy sauce
200 ml (7 fl oz) acacia honey
50 ml (1.7 fl oz) sushi vinegar
juice of 2 limes
10 ml (2 tsp) yuzu
1 lemongrass stalk
2 cloves of garlic
5 sprigs of thyme
a small piece of ginger
25 ml (0.9 fl oz) ginger syrup
3 star anise
50 g (1.8 oz) Sirop de Liège

60 g (2 oz) pulled lamb
30 g (1 oz) glaze
1 small hamburger bun
1 bunch of sage
fleur de sel
some dots of labneh yoghurt

Black garlic cream

basic mayonnaise (see p. 243)
4 cloves of black garlic

SPICY MERGUEZ

WITH HUMMUS AND BULGUR WHEAT

0.5 H

2 P

1 merguez sausage
1 pomegranate
5 black olives
a few sprigs of chervil

Hummus
300 g (10.5 oz) chickpeas
juice of 1 lime
100 ml (3.5 fl oz) chicken stock
(see p. 243)
75 g (2.5 oz) tahini

Bulgur wheat
70 g (2.5 oz) bulgur wheat
1 tbsp chardonnay vinegar
1 tbsp sushi vinegar
juice of ½ lime
salt and pepper
1 tbsp good olive oil
½ shallot
10 g (0.3 oz) chervil, finely chopped
10 g (0.3 oz) chives, finely chopped

Fry the merguez and cut into pieces.

Mix all the ingredients for the hummus until it has a smooth and creamy consistency.

Cook the bulgur wheat until al dente, cool, and combine with the other ingredients.

Garnish with the pomegranate seeds, finely chopped olives and a few sprigs of chervil.

PICKLED VEGETABLES

PICKLED CARROT AND CAULIFLOWER

Time: 30 minutes plus 1 month to develop the flavours. Quantity: 2–3 x 500 ml (17 fl oz) jars

4 carrots, half a cauliflower, 200 ml (7 fl oz) red wine vinegar, 200 ml (7 fl oz) water, 180 g (6.5 oz) brown sugar, 20 g (4 tsp) smoked sea salt, 1 star anise, 12 g (3 tsp) fennel seeds, 6 g (1 tsp) coriander seeds, 6 g (1 tsp) black peppercorns, preserving jars

Sterilise the preserving jars: submerge them in boiling water, then let them dry in the oven at 180°C (355°F).

Wash and peel the carrots and slice into coins. Cut the cauliflower into small florets and rinse well.

Boil the water, vinegar and sugar in a pan until the sugar has dissolved.

Toast the coriander and fennel seeds in a dry pan. Divide the spices, cauliflower and carrots evenly between the preserving jars. Push in firmly.

Pour the hot liquid over the vegetables until the jars are completely full. Screw on the lids, turn the jars upside down and back again, then store in a cool, dark place. Storage time: 1–2 months

PICKLED RED ONION

Time: 30 minutes plus a few days to develop the flavours. Quantity: 3 x 250 ml (9 fl oz) jars

400 g (14 oz) red onion, 300 ml (10.5 fl oz) red wine vinegar, 100 ml (3.5 fl oz) water, 250 g (9 oz) granulated sugar, 20 g (4 tsp) smoked sea salt, 1 star anise, 20 g (4 tsp) fennel seeds, 10 g (2 tsp) black peppercorns, preserving jars

Sterilise the preserving jars: submerge them in boiling water, then let them dry in the oven at 180°C (355°F).

Peel the red onion and cut into slices.

Boil the water, vinegar and sugar in a pan until the sugar has dissolved.

Divide the spices and onion slices evenly between the preserving jars. Pour over the hot liquid until the jars are completely full.

Screw on the lids, turn the jars upside down and back again, then store in a cool, dark place.
Storage time: 1–2 months

SPICED PICKLED CELERY

Time: 30 minutes plus a few days to develop the flavours. Quantity: 3 x 250 ml (9 fl oz) jars

300 g (10.5 oz) celery, 250 ml (9 fl oz) tarragon vinegar, 200 ml (7 fl oz) water, 300 g (10.5 oz) sugar, 1 star anise, 3 garlic cloves, 8 chilli peppers, 10 g (2 tsp) fennel seeds, 10 g (2 tsp) coriander seeds, 10 g (2 tsp) black peppercorns, preserving jars

Sterilise the preserving jars: submerge them in boiling water, then let them dry in the oven at 180°C (355°F)

Wash the celery and chop into pieces. Peel the garlic cloves. Toast the coriander and fennel seeds in a dry pan

Boil the water, vinegar and sugar in a pan until the sugar has dissolved.

Divide the garlic, chilli peppers, spices and celery evenly between the preserving jars. Pour over the hot liquid until the jars are completely full.

Screw on the lids, turn the jars upside down and back again, then store in a cool, dark place.
Storage time: 1–2 months

SWEET AND SOUR PICKLED RADISHES

Time: 30 minutes plus a few days to develop the flavours. Quantity: 3 x 250 ml (9 fl oz) jars

300 g (10.5 oz) radish, 250 ml (9 fl oz) cider vinegar, 200 ml (7 fl oz) water, 300 g (10.5 oz) sugar, 30 g (1 oz) smoked sea salt, 10 g (2 tsp) fennel seeds, 10 g (2 tsp) coriander seeds, 10 g (2 tsp) black peppercorns, preserving jars

Sterilise the preserving jars: submerge them in boiling water, then let them dry in the oven at 180°C (355°F)

Wash the radishes well. Remove the leaves and slice.

Boil the water, vinegar and sugar until the sugar has dissolved.

Place the radishes and spices in the preserving jars. Push the contents down firmly. Pour over the hot liquid until the jars are completely full.

Screw on the lids, turn the jars upside down and back again, then store in a cool, dark place. They need to steep for a few days to a month. Storage time: 1 month

CHICKEN STOCK

The secret to a tasty broth lies in the choice of chicken. Always opt for a free-range farm chicken.

Time: 4 hours – Quantity: 2 litres (3½ pints)

1 farm chicken (chopped), 1 knob of farm butter, 3 onions, 3 carrots, 1 leek, 3 celery stalks with leaves, 1 bouquet garni (parsley, thyme, bay leaf), 7 g (1½ tsp) black peppercorns, 2 litres (3½ pints) cold water

Wash and roughly chop the vegetables and crush the peppercorns. Heat the farm butter in a pan until it's golden brown. Gently sauté the onion, then add the rest of the vegetables and the herbs. Let this cook on a low heat for a while. Add the chopped chicken to the sautéed vegetables and cover with plenty of cold water.

Bring to a boil, reduce the heat and let it simmer gently for at least 2–3 hours, without a lid. Season with salt and pepper as needed. Occasionally skim off the foam with a slotted spoon. Strain the stock through a sieve lined with a tea towel. Let the stock cool, then remove the fat.

Store the stock in a fridge or freezer.

***Tip:** remove the chicken meat from the bones this is perfect for vol-au-vent or in a tasty salad.*

MAKING BRINE

The strength of a brine solution is measured on the Baumé scale.

Rule of thumb:
1 degree of Baumé = 12 g of sodium nitrite per 1 litre

Examples:
Do you have 4 litres of water and you want it to be 20° Baumé? Then this calculation applies:

4 × 20 × 12 = 960 g of sodium nitrite

Do you have 10 litres of water and you want it to be 10° Baumé?

10 × 10 × 12 = 1,200 g of sodium nitrite

BROWN FOND WITH BEEF OR VEAL

A fond is a reduced stock. This gives it a much more powerful flavour and makes it perfect for a wide range of sauces. If you let it reduce for a really long time, you get a glaze. You can brush the glaze on a shank or ribs for extra flavour.

Time: 6 hours
Quantity: 1–2 litres (1¾–3½ pints)

600 g (1 lb 5 oz) beef or veal shanks, oil, 3 carrots, 1 leek, 250 g (9 oz) celery, 2 onions, 15 g (1 tbsp) tomato purée, 1 bouquet garni (parsley, thyme, bay leaf), black peppercorns

Wash the vegetables and chop roughly. Crush the peppercorns. Rinse the shanks in cold water and pat them dry.

Heat some oil in a pan and brown the shanks (this can also be done in the oven).

Add the vegetables and cook for 10–20 minutes, stirring frequently. Add enough cold water to just cover. Bring to a simmer and cook gently for 3–4 hours, without a lid. Occasionally skim off the foam with a slotted spoon.

Strain the stock through a sieve lined with a tea towel. Let the stock cool, then remove the fat. If necessary, let it cook down for a while longer.

Store in the fridge or freezer for later.

PORK SKIN GELATINE

We often use gelatine leaves, or powder. Did you know that you can also make your own gelatine?

Time: 5 hours
Equipment: tea towel, strainer

Pork skins, calf's foot, vegetable stock

Place the calf's foot and pork skins in a pot. Cover in vegetable stock. Bring to a boil and simmer for 3–4 hours. Strain the broth.

Let the remaining liquid cool down a bit. Line the strainer with a tea towel and strain the liquid through. This is the gelatine.

VEGETABLE STOCK

Time: 2 hours – Quantity: 2 litres (3½ pints)

1 knob of farm butter, 3 onions, 3 carrots, 2 leeks, 2 tomatoes, 5 celery stalks, 1 bouquet garni (parsley, thyme, bay leaf), 7 g (1½ tsp) peppercorns, 30 ml (2 tbsp) oil, 1 sprig of rosemary, 3 garlic cloves, 2 litres (3½ pints) cold water

Wash and roughly chop the vegetables and crush the peppercorns. Heat the farm butter in a pan until it's golden brown. Gently sauté the onion, then add the rest of the vegetables and the herbs. Let this cook on a low heat for a while.

Add the water. Bring to a boil, reduce the heat and let it simmer gently for at least an hour, without a lid. Season with salt and pepper as needed. Occasionally skim off the foam with a slotted spoon.

Strain the stock through a sieve lined with a tea towel. Let the stock cool, then remove the fat.

Store the stock in a fridge or freezer.

MAYONNAISE

1 egg, 25 ml (0.9 fl oz) sushi vinegar, juice of 1 lime, 30 ml (1 fl oz) Forum chardonnay vinegar, a little pinch of xanthan gum, 1 tbsp mustard, a pinch of salt, 800 ml (28 fl oz) grapeseed oil and a splash of ice-cold water

Put all the ingredients except for the grapeseed oil into a blender or food processor. Blend for a few seconds, then slowly add the grapeseed oil until the mayonnaise reaches the desired thickness.

TASTE

CARCASSE LET'S START WITH THE BIGGEST CLICHÉ EVER: NEVER SAY NEVER.

HENDRIK DIERENDONCK VOWED THAT HE WOULD NEVER OPEN A RESTAURANT, AS IT IS AN ENTIRELY DIFFERENT WORLD FROM BUTCHERY, THE PROFESSION IN WHICH HE WAS BORN AND RAISED. SUPPLYING FINE MEAT PRODUCTS TO OTHER RESTAURANTS: NO PROBLEM. BUT OPENING ONE HIMSELF: NEVER! THERE'S MORE THAN ENOUGH WORK ALREADY. AT THE SAME TIME, HENDRIK IS SOMEONE WHO IS ALWAYS ON THE LOOKOUT FOR NEW OPPORTUNITIES. AND WHEN SUCH AN OPPORTUNITY PRESENTS ITSELF, HE GRABS IT WITH BOTH HANDS. SO WHEN A SPACE BECAME AVAILABLE EIGHT YEARS AGO NEXT TO HIS PARENTS' BUTCHER'S SHOP, HE DIDN'T HESITATE FOR A SECOND.

 AND THAT'S HOW THE BALL STARTED ROLLING...

RCASSE

"I WANTED TO OPEN A RESTAURANT THAT REFLECTS THE PHILOSOPHY OF OUR BUTCHER'S SHOP ON EVERY LEVEL."

In 2013, Hendrik spent a lot of time on the road giving butchery demos, workshops and so on. As his butchery business is at the Belgian seaside, it meant travelling far and wide and the journeys were often exhausting. Especially if you have to be back in your busy butcher's shop the next morning, feeling and looking fresh and lovely. Gradually, the long, long days started to take their toll. Until Hendrik realised that his newly acquired space could offer a solution. Initially, he intended to use it to hold tastings, demos, workshops and the now infamous 'Battle of the Butchers'. It was in early March 2013 that Hendrik crossed butcher's knives for the very first time with two French *confrères,* Yves-Marie Le Bourdonnec and Didier Massot, who are better known in their own country as *des bouchers* stars or top-class butchers. A fun and cutting-edge competition, between genuine and passionate craftsmen, to promote their noble profession. Designed to make the public think about the meat they eat, where it comes from, how it is cut and processed, and so on. "Meat, rock 'n roll style, a bit of good fun," as Hendrik says.

He started to mull over the idea of doing much more with this rather industrial space – including a boxing ring – behind the butcher's shop. But like his acclaimed meat, Hendrik's ideas need time to mature. Eighteen months, in this case.

When Hendrik finally sat down with his brother and architect Alexander, he knew exactly what he wanted and what he didn't. He wanted Alexander to redesign the tasting space into a fully fledged restaurant, but not another traditional restaurant. Ideally, he wanted a butcher's restaurant. Carcasse. The name as a starting point. No fuss; instead a concept that is very 'in your face'. Pure and simple. In mid January 2015, Carcasse finally opened its doors. In an excellent location on the corner of Koninklijke Baan and Henri Christiaenlaan in Sint-Idesbald. An extension of the Dierendonck butcher's shop in Strandlaan.

Anyone who comes to eat at Carcasse sits down at one of the long, inviting communal tables to enjoy the food that's about to be served. Traditional red and white checked kitchen towels are used in place of napkins. You can see the Josper charcoal grill in the open kitchen. A larger-than-life butcher's block, an antique slicing machine and the stainless-steel butcher's tables along the walls immediately catch the eye. The authentic atmosphere of a butcher's shop – carcasses, meat hooks, knives, cleavers, whole hams and white ceramic tiles – is immediately evident and blends seamlessly with the building's concrete walls and industrial vibe. The finishing touch is a rail on which the cuts of meat quarters can be pushed into the restaurant from the butcher's shop. It doesn't get more basic than this.

This unusual 'aorta' winds its way through the restaurant to what is essentially the beating heart of Carcasse: a floor-to-ceiling glass fridge, beautifully lit and showcasing the different breeds of meat on offer to customers. In some cases, the meat is cut in front of you, or you can watch the team as they prepare fresh black pudding. What you see is what you get. Here, the brute force of the muscular butcher – a pig's head is served at the table, and people are sometimes encouraged to eat with their hands – combines perfectly with the refinements of the master chef. Reconciling the irreconcilable. Or something like that. Now and then Hendrik likes to surprise his patrons with less obvious ingredients such as brains and kidneys, but they are always 'nicely packaged' and they come with a message. Nothing is done by chance at Carcasse. There is nothing accidental about what is served here, especially their own charcuterie.

The common theme is the Dierendoncks' now well-established nose-to-tail philosophy. This means not wasting anything, or, at least, as little as possible. And also: pointing this out to people. Making the customers think about what they're eating, if only for a minute. Compared with the past, we now eat much less – but much better – meat. We want to know where our meat comes from, how and where it was slaughtered, what has been done to it, and so on. Eating meat has become a tasting experience, as with wine or cheese. Hendrik always has an answer to relevant questions and is eager to share his extensive knowledge with everyone. Always passionate but never pedantic. Nothing in my hands, nothing up my sleeves.

"IN ADDITION TO MEAT LOVERS, MORE AND MORE FLEXITARIANS AND VEGETARIANS ARE FINDING THEIR WAY TO OUR RESTAURANT, WHICH OFFERS NEW PERSPECTIVES."

At Carcasse, and in the different workplaces, they are very serious about transparency. If you want to stretch your legs in between courses, and walk into the adjacent butcher's workplace or shop, to greet the staff and see what they're up to, then go ahead. And while you're there, choose a cut from the display that doesn't happen to be on the menu at Carcasse on that particular day. They will prepare it for you on the spot. The days when butchers were adamant about hiding their work from their customers with the excuse that "people don't eat meat anymore" are definitely over. Which is a good thing.

Whatever you do, don't use terms such as *saignant, à point* or *bien cuit.* They consider it tantamount to cursing. At Carcasse, all the meat is served *bleu chaud.* When you put that much time and effort into the meat, you can't afford to abuse it at the last minute on the grill or in the frying pan. That is why the restaurant doesn't serve french fries or béarnaise sauce either. While Hendrik doesn't mind them – on the contrary, he's an unconditional fan of traditional steak and chips – he wants to serve something different.

Above all, he's not interested in being on a collision course with the many restaurants to which he supplies meat. At Carcasse, the menu is limited to some starters and main courses with meat and vegetables. A lot of meat. And a lot of vegetables. Have you ever got up from a butcher's table feeling hungry? Well, then. It may sound strange, but flexitarians, or people who eat only chicken, and even full-blown vegetarians can always find something to their liking here, despite the fact that the restaurant essentially serves meat-based dishes.

The success of Carcasse got Hendrik thinking. Why not open a Carcasse in a large city such as Ghent or Brussels, where you have a completely different audience? Perhaps this would encourage the well-organised Dierendonck team to up its game and its working philosophy? Variety is the spice of life, after all. This is something to think about for the future. In general, Hendrik stocks meat from 15 or 16 different breeds. But he always offers a small selection in his restaurant, to make it easier for customers to decide – a long list of options is never good for the appetite. On the contrary. In the past six years, some of Carcasse's dishes have already become classics. The dish's name alone can whet your appetite. Just think of a dry-aged rib of beef or pastrami of Holstein beef. A smoked and cured delicacy that they would fight over in New York. Michelin-starred chef (and Hendrik's friend) Sergio Herman tasted pastrami for the first time at New York's legendary Katz's Deli and was immediately sold on the idea. But he just couldn't find pastrami with its typical crisp crust in Belgium. So Hendrik rose to the challenge, with a corned beef pâté, some spices and an air dryer. The result is a delicious crumble, comparable to beef jerky, which has become an essential ingredient in the Carcasse salads. Anything else, Sergio? It's just an example of how important the daily interaction between butcher and master chef has become. Here they have an open kitchen in every sense of the word.

'Open' as in unconditionally laying bare your inner soul. No unnecessary bluffing. Just lay all your trump cards on the table from the outset. And that is exactly what Hendrik Dierendonck does in this book. Providing a unique insight into the profession that has become his ultimate passion. As a breeder of West Flemish Red cattle and a butcher, a meat supplier and a master meat-ager, an occasional chef and a restaurant owner. And as the representative of the original Danish Butcher's Manifesto, a worldwide professional organisation of artisan butchers who believe in rehabilitating and preserving their profession where necessary. Based on specific ideas: innovation and tradition; a completely transparent meat industry; the transfer of knowledge; and responsible meat consumption. Values and norms that are perfectly suited to Hendrik. From nose to tail and from farm to table. A story that is never boring.

My dream has come true," says Hendrik. "I wanted to open a restaurant that reflects the philosophy of our butcher's shop on every level. Sitting at the table together, sharing dishes, sometimes with people you've never met before. That's what it's all about. I think Carcasse is the steak restaurant of the future. No sauces, no french fries, but beautiful and balanced side dishes full of seasonal vegetables. Working with chef Anthony Snoeck was a revelation and, together with restaurant manager Harm Rademan, I'm happy to say I can rely on a dream team. I want to further refine the creative ideas behind Carcasse. In addition to meat lovers, more and more flexitarians and vegetarians are finding their way to our restaurant, which offers new perspectives. This book is all about the future of meat, and how I envisage it as a butcher: always in combination with something else, always offset with tasty vegetables. It's the beginning of a great story, which still has a long way to go."

AFTER BEING THOROUGHLY RENOVATED, A FIFTH DIERENDONCK SHOP OPENED ITS DOORS IN UCCLE IN OCTOBER 2021. INCLUDING THE WEBSHOP, THE TOTAL NUMBER OF DIERENDONCK SHOPS NOW STANDS AT SIX.

HENDRIK DIERENDONCK WAS BORN AND RAISED IN A BUTCHER'S SHOP, THE PLACE WHERE HE STILL FEELS MOST AT HOME. AT THE SAME TIME, IT IS HIS GREATEST CHALLENGE. EVERYONE WHO STANDS BEHIND THE COUNTER OR IN THE ATELIER MUST DISPLAY THE SAME PASSION AND PHILOSOPHY THAT ARE SO MUCH PART OF HIS CHARACTER. "WITHOUT PASSION YOU CAN'T CONVEY THE MESSAGE TO YOUR CUSTOMERS IN THE STORE," HE SAYS. "THAT'S EXACTLY WHAT NEEDS TO BE DONE THERE, AND WITH A SENSITIVE EYE FOR DETAIL. EACH HEAD BUTCHER IS GIVEN A CERTAIN FREEDOM, BUT I MAKE SURE THAT THE PASSION FOR THE PRODUCTS WE SELL IS ALWAYS THERE. I THINK OF A BUTCHER'S SHOP AS A SWEET SHOP FOR GROWN-UPS, ESPECIALLY IN TODAY'S 'LESS BUT BETTER' ERA. WHATEVER YOU THINK OF IT, WE ARE MOVING TOWARDS A TIME IN WHICH MEAT IS GOING TO BE A PREMIUM PRODUCT. THAT IS WHY I TRY TO DELIVER SOMETHING UNIQUE IN ALL OUR SHOPS, WHERE TRANSPARENCY, SERVICE AND CUSTOMER-FRIENDLINESS ARE OF THE UTMOST IMPORTANCE. WHATEVER THE CONTENTS, THE PACKAGE THAT YOU HAND OVER TO THE CUSTOMER SHOULD ALWAYS FEEL LIKE A PRESENT."

Mangalica
The Netherlands 28 days
France 35 days
France 28 jours
Côte à l'os Maine-Anjou
Spain 42 days
Côte à l'os Rubia Galega
England 28 days
Côte à l'os Hereford
€45.00 kg
Melklamsbout Pyreneeën Gigot d'agneau
€54.50 kg

CONTREFILET LIMOUSIN
CÔTE À L'OS WEST VLAAMS ROOD RUND
5 WEKEN
54,85€/kg

"I THINK OF A BUTCHER'S SHOP AS A SWEET SHOP FOR GROWN-UPS."

COLOPHON

Text
Hendrik Dierendonck, Marijke Libert, René Sépul and Stijn Vanderhaeghe

Translation
Elise Reynolds

Editing
Cath Phillips

Photography
Thomas Sweertvaegher, except:

Stephan Vanfleteren
(pp. XII-XIII, XIV-XV, XX-XXI, XXVI-XXVII, XXX-XXXI, XXXIV-XXXV, XXXVIII-XXXIX)

Piet Dekersgieter
(pp. 80-81, 82, 84-85, 114-115, 116, 118, 119, 120-121, 122-123, 142-143, 145, 151, 152, 155, 156, 161, 182, 185, 186, 210, 219, 239, 240, 244-245, 248, 251)

Pieter D'Hoop (pp. 94, 108-109, 110, 112-113)
Gazeuse – Toon Stockman (pp. 246-247, 254-255)
Dierendonck (pp. 252, 253)
Séverine Lacante (endpapers, pp. 86-87)

Illustrations
Gaston de Lapoyade – for Gazeuse (cover (logo), pp. 96-97, 166-167, 230-231)

Project manager
Hadewych Van den Bossche

Art direction
Natacha Hofman

Design
Johan Jacobs

Printing
die Keure, Bruges, Belgium

Binding
Brepols, Turnhout, Belgium

ISBN 978 94 6388 794 6
D/2021/11922/31
NUR 440

www.hannibalbooks.be
HANNIBAL

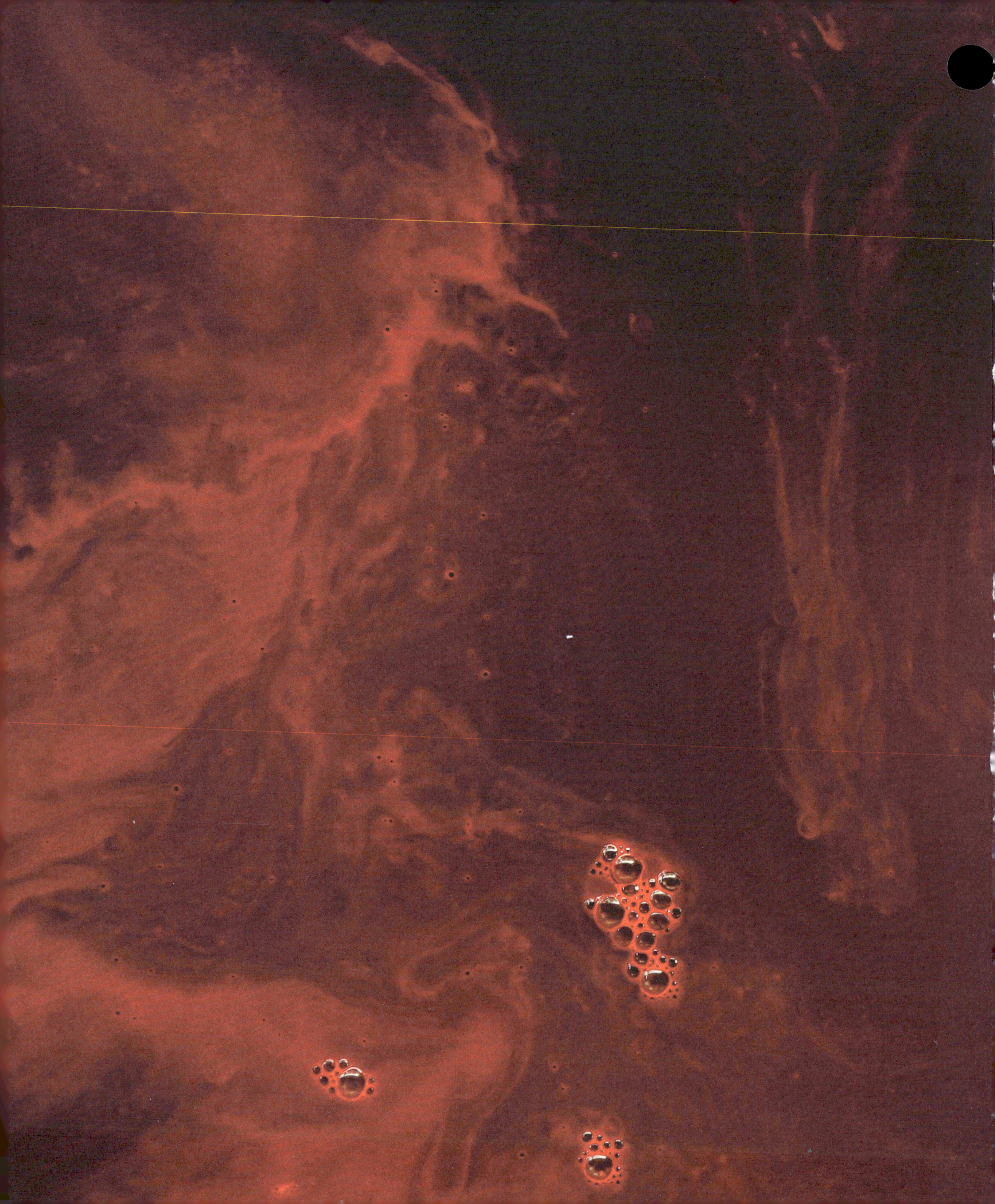